# *Passion* ON THE CUTTING BOARD

## SWEET, SALTY, SPICY & EVERYTHING IN BETWEEN

## CHEF RENEE BLACKMAN

**PHOTOGRAPHY BY**
**RENEE BLACKMAN, MARTA SKOVRO**
**NICK FINOCHIO & JASMERA LAWSON**

# CONTENTS

**FOREWORD**
7

**FOOD IS LOVE**
9

**INTRODUCTION**
10

**ACKNOWLEDGMENTS**
177

**A LITTLE BREKKIE**
17

**GRAB A PLATE**
104

**THINGS WE ORDER AT BRUNCH**
32

**SWEET FINALE**
130

**A FRESH TAKE**
64

**LIBATIONS**
154

**LOVE ON YOUR PUP**
166

"Enjoy Life and break bread amongst friends"
– Chef Renée

**Barbados Food & Rum Festival 2024**
Roasted corn gnocchi w/ flank steak, honey chive emulsion, coconut garlic cream and crispy thyme lentil gremolata.

# FOREWORD

I met Chef Renee Blackman in 2019 when she was one of the featured chefs for my first "Caribbean Tradishon" dinner at the James Beard House. I remember the way she entered the kitchen; poised, militant, and completely in command of her craft, like the three-time champion choir in Sister Act 2. At that moment, I knew she was a force to be reckoned with.

At the end of the night, as the last dishes were cleared and the final toast was made, Renee turned to me, completely satisfied with how everything had unfolded. She looked me in the eye and said, "Nneka, you executed the six P's with precision."

Curious, I asked, "What's that?"

She smiled and replied, "Proper Preparation Prevents a Piss Poor Performance."

That moment solidified our connection because, unbeknownst to her, my father had always drilled into me: If you fail to prepare, prepare to fail. It was then I knew Renee was my soul sister, or, as she likes to call me, her "Sister Mummy," driven by the same principles of excellence and execution.

For the past two years, Renee has been meticulously crafting this cookbook, Passion on the Cutting Board. As her cooking style evolved, so did her desire to bring that same passion into people's homes. Coming out of the pandemic, there was a void, a missing connection between home kitchens and the elevated dining-out and comfort food experience. Renee had the antidote. She knew her audience, and more importantly, she knew how to equip them with the tools to cook with confidence, even with minimal kitchen experience.

What makes Passion on the Cutting Board even more special is that Renee isn't classically trained—and that fresh perspective shines through. She curated dishes with the home cook in mind, ensuring that every recipe is accessible, achievable, and impactful, whether for an intimate dinner for two or a lively gathering with family and friends.

This cookbook is a direct connection to Chef Renee's world, her passion, and her creative vision. Her ability to craft intricate, restaurant-worthy dishes while making them approachable for the home cook is what sets this book apart. It's more than a collection of recipes; it's an experience, an invitation to elevate your culinary skills while embracing the joy of cooking.

So, as you turn these pages, prepare to step into the world of Chef Renee Blackman and her elevated comfort food. A woman with the warmest smile, the sharpest knives, and an unwavering commitment to delivering the absolute best performance in the kitchen.

Enjoy the journey, and may your cutting board always be filled with passion.

- **Nneka Nurse**

# FOOD IS LOVE

There's something special about savoring each bite, enjoying good company and appreciating the time and effort that bring us together at the table. When I began cooking, I realized I shared the patience of my grandmother Hazel and my mum in the kitchen; a dash of this, a little of that, infused with laughter and a deep sense of fulfillment.

Looking back, no one warned me that trailing behind my grandmother in Barbados would lead me to emulate her, eventually falling in love with food as I did with her. Yes, her! As I write this with a smile on my face, I realize she was the first woman I was truly smitten by. She nurtured my connection with food, something I could grasp and hold onto.

Maybe I've always enjoyed working with my hands, but I found joy in the simplest tasks, picking peas from the backyard and sifting rice by hand to remove the discolored grains. Some days, I tried to be helpful by gathering mangos and breadfruit. I remember wielding a tall piece of bamboo with a knife tied to the end with twine. Imagine a seven year old me, waving that stick in the air, hoping to pull down a breadfruit. It was such a failure.

I think of the Friday nights when my mum made burgers and popped popcorn on the stove for my brother Corey and I, while we watched movies. Such beautiful moments replay in my mind. My mum would bake her heart out every holiday! Her sweet bread was always my favorite, fresh out of the oven. Her pone, cupcakes and black cake. OMG! That black cake was everything to me.

There are countless stories tied to my journey with food, each one a thread in the fabric of who I am. Please enjoy a piece of me as I bare my soul on the cutting board.

# INTRODUCTION

Nostalgia is a powerful and deeply personal experience. A familiar song or the scent of a favorite dish can transport us back to cherished moments, stirring memories of the people and places that shaped us. These fleeting emotions invite us to pause, savoring the warmth they bring before they fade.

For me, food will always be my gateway to comfort and joy. I think of my mom's fish cakes though to this day, I couldn't tell you exactly what she puts in the batter. Maybe it's the well seasoned pot or the magic in her hands, but the aroma of her cooking instantly takes me back to my childhood in Barbados. Back then, those fish cakes were always paired with a cold glass of Pine Hill Dairy's passion fruit juice.

It's funny how our fondest memories so often unfold around a meal or a cocktail, with laughter echoing between bites and sips. Every dish carries a story, a connection, a moment waiting to be revived. This collection of recipes is more than just food; it's a tribute to the people who hold a special place in my heart and the memories we've created together.

# THE AROMATICS OF HERBS

Herbs can be used in a variety of ways from seasoning meats, infusing oils, compound butters, syrups for cocktails and can even be used in desserts.

- **Fresh herb Pairings frequently used:**
- **Basil, oregano, rosemary parsley & sage - Italian**
- **Mint, oregano, dill & chives - Mediterranean**
- **Thai Basil, mint & cilantro - Thai & Vietnamese**
- **Cilantro & oregano - Spanish**
- **Parsley, thyme, marjoram, coriander - West Indian**

Whether used whole or finely chopped, herbs make a great addition to flavor profile and appearance of many dishes.

Releasing the fragrant oils of these herbs are relatively easy and can add an elevated taste to your dishes. Hold a few leaves together and twist, slightly bruising the leaves. If you desire to get more of the aromatics, rub them in the palm of your hands for a few seconds to release the oils.

My favorite magical dried herb mix to keep on hand for roasted vegetables or roasted chicken is Herbs de Provence. This seasoning of thyme, basil, rosemary, tarragon, lavender, savory, marjoram and oregano builds a beautiful flavor.

If you're looking for a quick way to dry out your herbs, grab a plate and place a paper towel down, spread your herbs out and microwave in 30 second increments for 2 minutes until dried out. Allow to cool and store in an airtight container.

# DON'T SWEAT THE TECHNIQUES

These simple techniques can truly determine the outcome of a dish. Think about where you are headed and what you're making. Cooking can be fun and simple when taking the time to remember "Food is love".

**Searing -** Searing meat is about building flavor and obtaining a beautiful crust on your protein. Using a pan with controlled mid to high heat, add a thin layer of oil to the pan. Once the oil is hot, place your meat in the pan and enjoy the sizzle , don't crowd the pan and don't fuss with the food, give it a chance to caramelize.

**Roasting -** Let your oven do the work on this one. Place your marinated proteins or seasoned vegetables in a roasting pan or sheet pan, Preheat your oven to 350 degrees, set your timer and let the oven roast and caramelize , carefully rotate your pan halfway through the cooking process for even results.

**Broiling -** Use of the broiler is a finishing technique that can give your vegetables or meats a nice char when you can't get outside to the grill.

**Slow cooking -** Slow and steady wins the race when it comes to this practice. It's perfect for tough cuts of meat or braising vegetables at 225 to 275 degrees for a few hours in a covered baking dish or pot.

**Brining -** To brine or not to brine? Brining is one of the best things you can do to poultry or fish and yes I said fish! Submerging the protein in an extremely flavored water bath for 2 hours or overnight, will be slightly tenderized and superbly flavored.

**Marinating -** Marinades call for food to be coated in seasonings, acidity and oil.

**Tempering -** Tempering is the process of combining two liquids of different temperatures. The liquids are slowly combined to gradually become the same temperature.

**Air Drying -** drying of meats & fish in a low moisture chilled area. This process can be done at home in the refrigerator by holding proteins for 24 - 72 hrs. Allowing the air to make contact with the protein, which allows for a crispy skin.

# QUICK REFERENCES FOR THE SUCCESSFUL COOK

When a little of this and a little of that just won't cut it, these tips will help you make date night or whatever night a great one.

**Salt -** My recipes call for kosher salt, nothing against sea salt, Himalayan, black salt or table salt but, it's a hard NO for me.

**House Mix -** Keep this on hand for literally everything, equal parts kosher salt, coarse ground pepper and granulated garlic, blend with a whisk and place in an airtight container.

**Roux -** Roux is made from equal parts of flour and butter by weight. Using a saucepan, melt 1 part butter and slowly stir in 1 part flour, stirring for 5 - 10 minutes. Roux is best used to thicken sauces such as stews or bechamel frequently used for Mac n Cheese.

**Cornstarch slurry -** Combining water and cornstarch, this can be added to drippings to make gravy, sauces, stews or soups to thicken.

**Compound butter -** Softened butter with additions of herbs, truffles, shallots or citrus. Great for finishing steaks or adding to seafood.

**Roasted garlic -** The more the merrier in my opinion, cut the top off a garlic bulb, drizzle with olive oil and sprinkle some kosher salt, wrap in foil and roast in the oven for 45 minutes at 400 degrees until it's soft. Perfect with steak or adding to mashed potatoes.

# THE 1,2,3's...

**Rice -** Here's a tip for parboiled, brown rice, jasmine and basmati rice. Rinse your rice prior to cooking. Using a bowl with water, rub the grains in your hands, you will notice the water becoming somewhat milky or cloudy and you rinse the rice. Strain through a sieve and repeat until the water runs clear. Grab a heavy bottomed pot with a matching lid, always use a 2:1 ratio. 1 part rice, 2 parts water, add a pinch of salt, place on low and cook for 30 mins until cooked, use a fork to give the rice and fluff.

**Pasta -** Bring water to a rolling boil in a pot and cook your dried pasta for 9 minutes. Be sure to heavily salt the water. For best results, pull the pasta out of the water while slightly al dente. Toss in olive oil to prevent sticking if you intend on leaving it plain. This method works when using orzo or smaller pastas.

**Quinoa -** Tricky but completely worth the effort. Rinse the quinoa using a sieve to remove residue, you'll notice that it appears foamy. Place the quinoa in a pot and cover with water, on low heat, allow the quinoa to cook and fluff lightly, at this point, you can add oil, herbs and any seasonings.

**Mashed potatoes -** This can go south if you aren't a potato specialist. Peel your potatoes and cut in quarters, add to a pot of water and bring to a boil. Allow the potatoes to cook thoroughly, until fork tender, strain and allow all the potatoes to dry out a bit and return to the pot. Using another pot, heat, heavy cream and butter. Mash the potato with a masher or ricer using a bit of elbow grease, add salt to taste and add the creamed butter mix slowly folding until it has a silky, yet light consistency.

# A Little Brekkie

# Bacon Egg N' Cheese

*Serves:* 1  *Prep time:* 25 min  *Total time:* 25 min

1 Kaiser Roll
2 eggs beaten
1 tbsp scallions thinly chopped
1 slice white cheddar cheese
3 - 4 slices of bacon from the bacon Gods
Pinch of salt
Pinch of coarse ground pepper

Cook the bacon in the oven at 400 degrees for 20 minutes (Carefully flip to the other side at the 10 minute mark and continue to cook for another 10 minutes)

Crack the eggs in a bowl, add scallions, salt and pepper and then beat heavily.

Slice your roll in half and lightly butter both sides.

Using a skillet, toast the roll lightly and set to the side.

Using the same pan add ½ tbsp of butter and ½ tsp vegetable oil. Once the pan is hot, add the eggs and let them cook on medium heat for 1 ½ - 2 minutes. Add the cheese and cover the pan so it gets melty, shmelty!

Be sure to turn off the heat and immediately place the eggs and bacon on the toasted bun, with a bit of garlic aioli **(See page 55)** on the top bun, cut in half and enjoy with a cup of ice cold orange juice.

# Cinnamon Rolls

***Serves:*** *10*  ***Prep time:*** *1 hr 45 min*  ***Total time:*** *2 hr 20 min*

**Dough**
3 cups of flour
1 egg
2 tbsp sugar
7 grams instant yeast
3 tbsp brown butter
1 cup of milk (warm)
1 tsp kosher salt
¼ heavy cream (reserve until ready to bake)

**Filling**
2 tbsp cinnamon
1 cup brown sugar
3/4 cup freshly shaved coconut
1 ½ tsp cornstarch
6 tbsp brown butter
1 tsp almond extract

**Frosting**
6 oz cream cheese (room temp)
3 tbsp butter (room temp)
2 tbsp milk
1 cup powdered sugar
1 tsp almond extract
½ tsp salt

Add all ingredients, except the flour and salt to the stand mixer.

Using the hook attachment on low to medium speed add each cup of flour slowly to incorporate for 8 minutes. Add the salt with the final cup of flour.

This will create a slightly sticky dough. The dough will pull from the side but still stick to the bottom. **DON'T** add anymore flour!

Lightly grease a metal bowl and scrape the dough into it. Cover with plastic wrap for an hour in a warm place. (A microwave always works best.)

While the dough is rising, make your filling. Add the cinnamon, coconut, brown sugar, cornstarch to a bowl, mix thoroughly and set aside.

For the frosting, combine the butter and cream cheese, ensuring there are no lumps. Add the milk, powdered sugar, salt and almond extract, combine until smooth and set aside.

Once the hour mark has passed, lightly flour a clean surface and rolling pin. Turn out the dough onto a floured surface and roll out the dough into a 12 x 18 rectangle.

Spread the butter and filling across the surface leaving ½ inch room at the edge. Roll the dough tightly and cut 1 ¼ inch rolls with unwaxed floss or a sharp knife.

Lay upwards in a greased baking dish, cover lightly with plastic wrap and allow to rise for 45 minutes and not a minute more!!!!

Pour ¼ cup of warm heavy cream over the proofed rolls. ( keeps the rolls moist and assists in a silky mouthfeel while indulging.

Bake at 350 for 15 -16 minutes (while golden brown deliciousness is standard for baked goods, we are also aiming for thoroughly cooked, moist and flavorful cinnamon rolls!)

Once removed from the oven, allow to cool for a few minutes, spread the frosting and enjoy.

# Avocado Toast W/ Smoked Salmon & Brown Butter Ricotta

*Serves:* 2     *Prep time:* 10 min     *Total time:* 15 min

---

4 oz Smoked Salmon
2 slices sourdough bread
1 avocado
1 Lime
1 tbsp minced cilantro
¼ finely diced onion
2 tbsp butter
½ cup of ricotta
1 tbsp hot honey
1 tsp red pepper flakes
1 tbsp crushed pistachios
pinch of salt
lemon Zest
1 tbsp olive oil

**Perfect guac**
1 avocado
Juice of ½ lime
1 tsp kosher salt
1 tbsp finely chopped jalapeno pepper
1 ½ tsp finely chopped cilantro

To brown the butter, place in a small saucepan on low heat until browned, keeping a watchful eye. Allow to cool and strain over ricotta, add salt and the zest of ½ lemon, stir until combined.

Thoroughly mash the avocado, onion, cilantro, lime juice and add a pinch of salt.

Slice the sourdough into ½ inch cuts and drizzle with olive oil.

Using a skillet on medium heat toast on both sides and allow to cool.

Spread the guac on the toasted sourdough, place small spoonfuls of the ricotta over different sections of the toast and layer the smoked salmon.

Drizzle the hot honey, crushed pistachios, red pepper flakes, and fresh shaved lemon zest for freshness on top of the toast

# Quiche Loraine

*Serves:* 6     *Prep time:* 1 hr     *Total time:* 1.5 hr

**Dough**
2 ¼ cup all purpose flour
2 sticks unsalted butter
1 tsp kosher Salt
1 tsp sugar
8 tbsp ice cold water

**Filling**
4 eggs
Heavy cream
5 strips of thick cut bacon
1/2 medium onion diced
1 tsp thyme
½ tsp kosher Salt
½ tsp black pepper
Few dashes of hot sauce
1 cup cheddar cheese
Few shavings of nutmeg

Using a food processor, add the flour, sugar, salt and butter and pulse until a flaky crumb forms. Slowly add the water and pulse until fully combined and forms a ball.

Remove from the food processor and divide into two 4 inch rounds. You won't need both, but why not have extra pie dough for another wonderful quiche?

Wrap each round in plastic wrap and refrigerate for 30 minutes.

Flour your work surface and rolling pin. Roll the dough out on a lightly floured surface starting from the center and returning, moving in opposing directions.

In the event your dough edges split, simply pinch it together and continue the process.

Pick up the dough using the rolling pin. Start from one edge and roll the dough towards you. Place in your baking dish and crimp the edges as you see fit. Place the dough back in the fridge for 20 minutes and preheat your oven to 375 degrees.

Blind bake in the oven for 20 minutes. Fully cover the center and edges. (you can put pie weights or another baking dish, very similar in size to weigh down the bottom of the pie, preventing the dough from baking unevenly).

To make your filling, saute the bacon for 6-8 minutes until cooked, remove from the pan and place on a paper towel, discard the majority of the bacon fat, keeping a tbsp of it to saute the onion until translucent.

Beat the eggs, hot sauce, cream, thyme, nutmeg, salt and pepper. Place the cheese, bacon and onion in the pie crust and pour the egg mix over the top.

Bake for 325 degrees for 35 minutes, allow to cool slightly before handling.

# Sweet Potato Oatmeal Pancakes

*Serves:* 2  *Prep time:* 35 min  *Total time:* 40 min

**Pancake Batter**
1 cup sweet Potato
1 ½ cup rolled oats
1 tsp cinnamon
⅛ tsp nutmeg
1 tsp kosher salt
2 eggs
1 cup of milk
1 1/4 tsp baking powder
1 tsp baking soda
1 tbsp brown sugar
1 tsp freshly shaved ginger
1 tsp vanilla extract
Butter to cook

**Whipped ricotta**
½ cup ricotta
⅓ cup yogurt
1 tbsp honey
½ tsp cinnamon

Roast the sweet potato for 30 minutes in a 350 degree oven, allowing it to cool before adding to the blender. (This can be done the night before to quicken the process).

Add the oats to a blender and blend until the oats become fine.

Add the remaining ingredients and blend until fully combined. There will still be a bit of texture.

Heat a skillet on medium to low heat.

Add a sliver of butter & allow it to slowly melt before adding batter each time you form a pancake.

Cook for 2 minutes on low to medium heat.

You'll know the pancakes are ready to flip once you see tiny little bubbles.

Flip and cook for an additional 2 minutes. If you're looking for those crispy edges, add a bit of butter and swirl around the pancake.

Friendly tip, don't over work your batter and wipe the pan every 2 to 3 pancakes as the butter burns.

Using a small bowl, add all of the ingredients for the whipped ricotta and bring together. Place on top of your finished pancakes.

# Sneaky Apple Pie

*Serves:* 2    *Prep time:* 10 min    *Total time:* 12 min

---

2 granny smith apples
3 tbsp brown sugar
1 tsp cinnamon
1 tsp cornstarch
⅓ cup of water
Few shavings of nutmeg

**Whipped ricotta**
½ cup ricotta
⅓ cup yogurt
1 tbsp honey
½ tsp cinnamon

**Topping**
1/4 cup granola (your favorite protein based brand)

Peel and slice the granny smith apples thinly.

In a bowl combine the apples, cornstarch, cinnamon, sugar and nutmeg. Toss together until the apples are completely coated.

Using a skillet, add the apple mix and the water on a medium heat and allow the apples to cook for 10 minutes, until fork tender.

Remove from the heat and divide into 2 plates.

Using a small bowl add all of the ingredients for the whipped ricotta and bring together.

Garnish with your favorite granola and the whipped ricotta.

Serve immediately.

To make this recipe vegan friendly, use vegan sour cream & ricotta in place of the yogurt and ricotta.

# The Dutch Baby

*Serves:* 3-4   *Prep time:* 10 min        *Total time:* 45 min

**Batter**
2 eggs
1/2 cup flour
3 tbsp sugar
1 tsp vanilla extract
1/2 cup milk
1/2 tsp kosher salt

**Brandied blueberries**
½ pint of blueberries
½ cup sugar
Juice of half a lemon
1/tsp of brandy

**Devonshire cream**
3 tbsp cream cheese
1 cup heavy cream
1 1/2 tbsp sugar
1 tsp vanilla

Lemon zest( reserved for topping)

Heat the oven to 375 degrees and put the cast iron skillet in the oven for 15 minutes.

Add 3 tbsp of butter once the pan is hot and swirl around to fully coat. Return to the oven for 2 minutes.

For the batter, add all ingredients into a blender and blend until fully combined.

Pour it into the hot pan, don't worry if butter comes over the sides (it's wonderful and we want that interesting shape) Bake for 20 mins.

While the dutch baby is in the oven, lightly macerate the blueberries for 5 minutes adding all ingredients to a small pot on a medium heat. Remove from the heat and cool.

For the cream, make sure the cream cheese is room temperature. Whip the cream cheese and sugar together, then add the heavy cream and vanilla. Keep chilled until ready to use.

Once the dutch baby is finished, allow it to cool for 10 minutes before adding the cream and blueberries. Add some zest for added freshness.

Chili lime quinoa w/ corn salsa & Peruvian bbq spiced shrimp

# Things we order at brunch

# Shakshuka w/ Fried Fish

*Serves:* 1  *Prep time:* 20 min  *Total time:* 1 hr

---

3 flounder fillets halved
1 lime
2 cups water

**Fish Seasoning**
1 tsp kosher salt
1 tsp granulated garlic
½ tsp old bay
1 tbsp green seasoning **(See page 50)**
1 tbsp olive oil

**Fish Dredge**
1 cup all purpose flour
2 tbsp cornstarch
1 tbsp kosher salt
1 tbsp paprika
1 tsp onion powder
1 tbsp lemon pepper
1 tbsp granulated garlic
1 tbsp cornmeal

**Tomato Sauce**
2 tbsp olive oil
4 roma tomatoes
½ green pepper diced
½ medium onion diced
3 cloves of garlic sliced
1 cup crushed tomatoes
1 tbsp red wine vinegar
1 tbsp cumin
1 tbsp herb de provence
1 tbsp sugar
2 tbsp salt
1 tsp coarse black pepper
1 tsp red pepper flakes (optional)
1 tsp smoked paprika
3 - 4 eggs

Soak the flounder in lime and water for 30 minutes

Pat the fillets dry and season with kosher salt, garlic, old bay, green seasoning and olive oil.

Using medium heat add 2 tbsp of olive oil to a saute pan and add the onion, green pepper, garlic and tomatoes. Saute for 2 minutes and add the seasonings and tomato sauce. Simmer for 25 minutes, gradually stirring the sauce.

Using the back of a spoon make an indentation for the eggs. Crack the eggs separately and gently place them in the perfect spot. Cover and cook for 7-8 minutes. The longer the cook time, the less runny your eggs will be.

Heat a pot of oil on a medium heat to fry the fish. Dredge in fish mix, shaking off the excess.

Fry the fish for 2 - 3 minutes.

Serve immediately and enjoy.

# The Unforgettable Potato

**Serves:** 1   **Prep time:** 25 min   **Total time:** 1 hr

1 large baking potato
Oil to fry

**Cheese sauce**
1 tbsp butter
1 tbsp flour
1 dash of hot sauce
1 tsp dijon mustard
¼ cup heavy cream
⅓ cup cheddar

**Spice Mix**
⅓ tsp paprika
½ granulated garlic
1 tsp kosher salt
½ tsp cumin
½ tsp onion powder
½ tsp sugar

Sprinkle of furikake
1 tsp crunchy garlic crisp
(this can be found in your local Asian market)
Scallions

Peel and cut your potato into 1 inch cubes.

Boil for 20 minutes. Strain and chill for 25 minutes.

Cut your scallions on a bias into 1.5 inch strips, cut thinly and soak in ice water to curl.

Using a small saucepan, melt the butter and add the flour, creating a light roux for 5 minutes. Add the cream, cheese, hot sauce and mustard. Whisk until smooth.

Heat a pot with oil on a medium heat. Carefully place the potato into the oil and fry for 7 minutes.

Once the potato is fried, add to a bowl and toss with the spice mix.

Top with the cheese sauce, furikake, chili crisp and scallion.

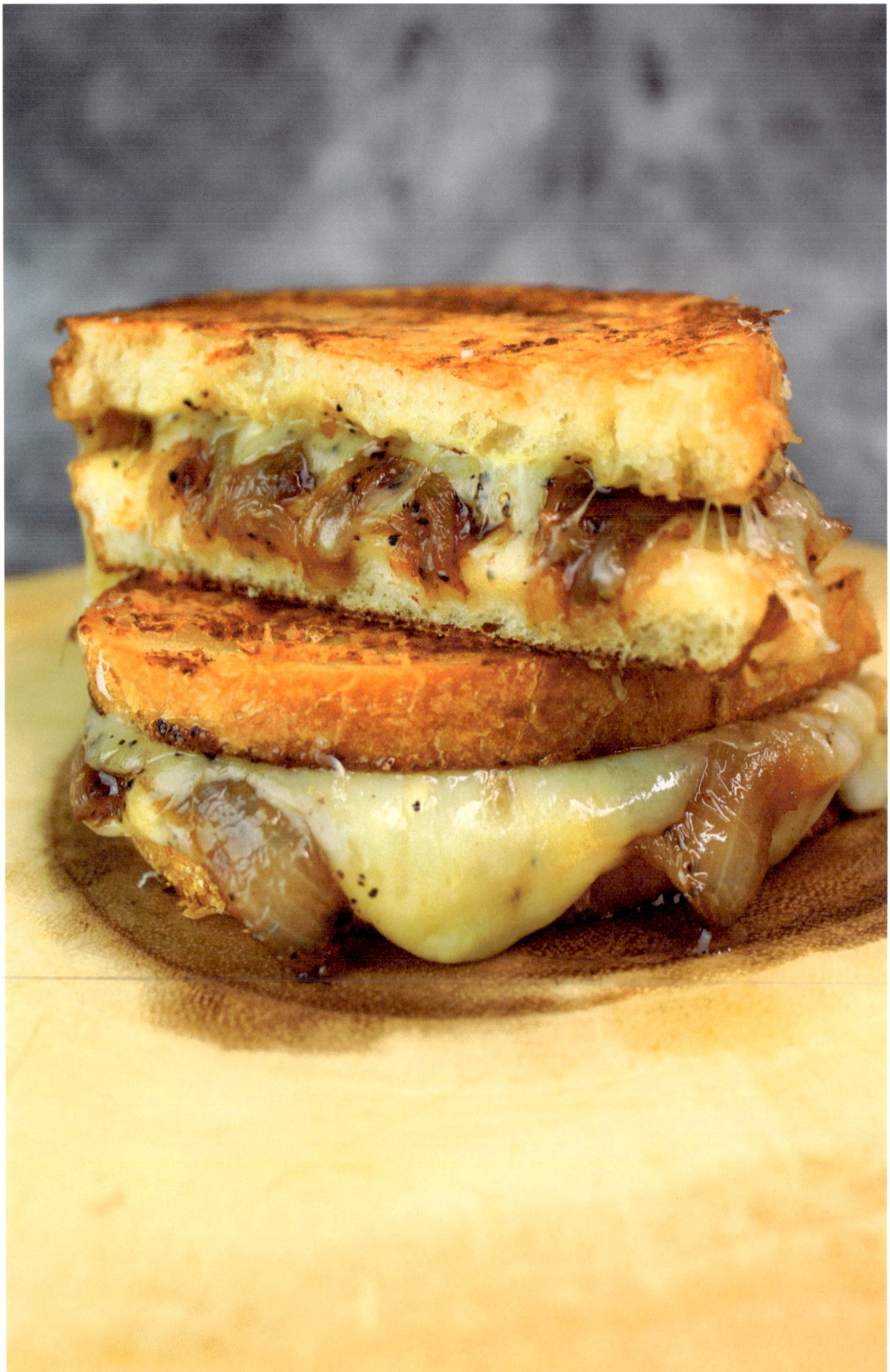

# The 3 AM Grilled Cheese

*Serves:* 1     *Prep time:* 10 min     *Total time:* 25 min

2 slices of sourdough bread
½ small onion, thinly sliced
1 slice of havarti cheese
1 slice of cheddar cheese
1 tsp chopped thyme
1 tsp balsamic vinegar
1 tbsp honey
Pinch of salt
1 tbsp dijon mustard
1 tsp black pepper
Light drizzle of Truffle oil
1 tbsp Mayo
2 tbsp butter (room temp)
Fresh parmesan

Using medium heat add a tbsp of butter to a saute pan and add the thinly sliced onion.

Saute the onions for 7 minutes, add the balsamic vinegar, honey, black pepper, salt and thyme and saute for an additional 2 minutes.

Add a tsp of truffle oil, stir and remove from the heat.

Using the same pan, rub the bread in the remnants of the onion juices.

Place the bread on the cutting board with the sides you rubbed in the onion facing up towards you.

Spread the dijon mustard on both sides. Place the havarti cheese on one side and cheddar cheese on the other, spread the sauteed onion evenly and close the sandwich.

Mix the remaining butter and mayo together, spread on both sides of the bread and grate fresh parmesan on both sides.

Using a skillet, cook for 2-3 minutes on low heat.

Remove from the heat, cut in half and enjoy.

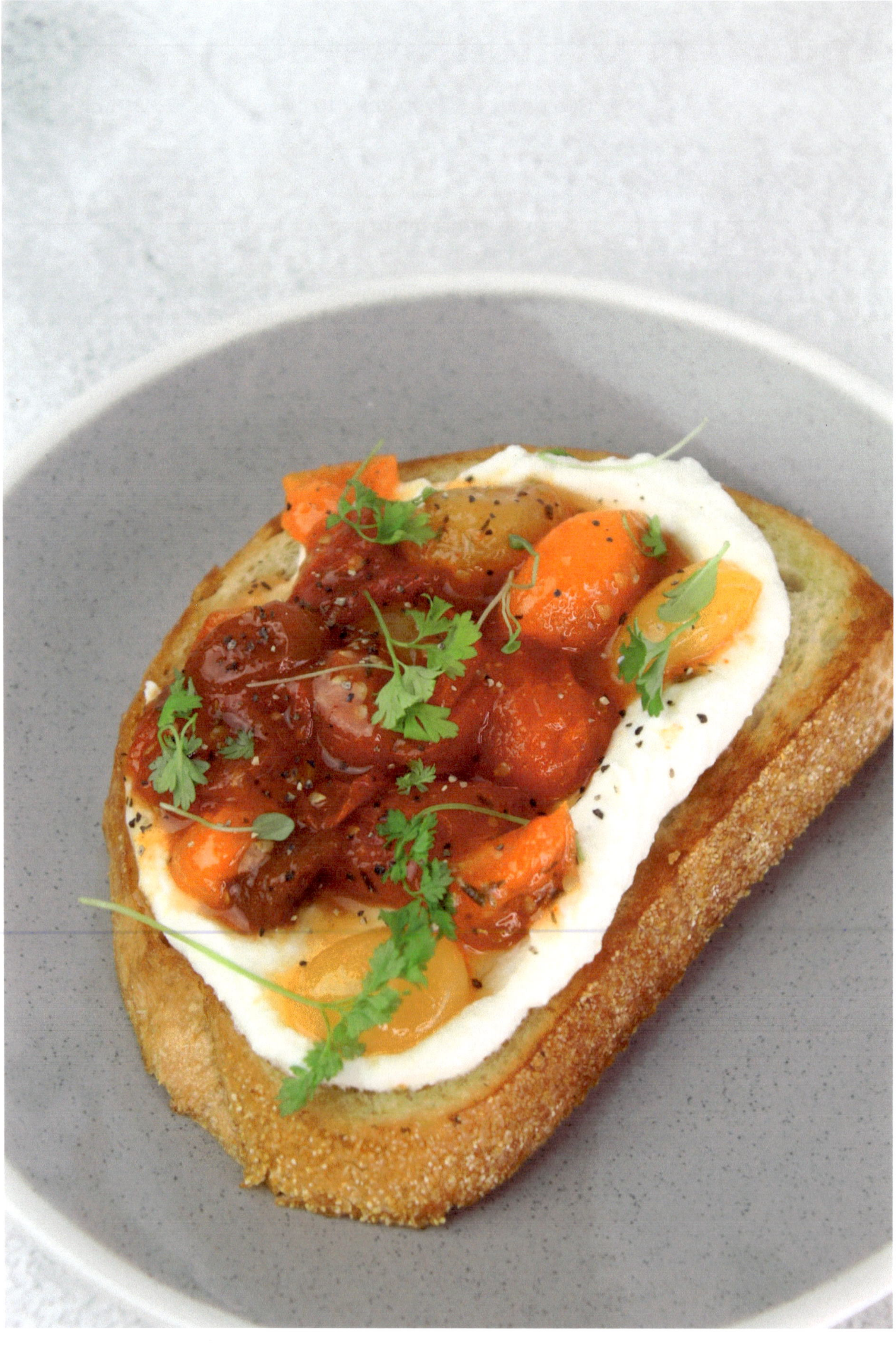

# Candied Tomato Bruschetta

*Serves:* 2  *Prep time:* 20 min  *Total time:* 35 min

2 slices of sourdough bread
Olive oil to toast

**Brown butter ricotta**
1 ½ tbsp butter
½ cup of ricotta
Zest of ½ a lemon
1 tbsp heavy cream
½ tsp salt

**Candied tomato**
½ tsp herb de provence
1 ½ cup cherry tomatoes halved
½ tsp granulated garlic
1 ½ tbsp vinegar
⅛ tsp cayenne pepper
3 tbsp sugar
½ tsp salt

Cut the cherry tomatoes in half and add to a small pot.

Add the salt, garlic, cayenne, herb de provence, sugar and rice wine vinegar to the cherry tomatoes and cook on a low to medium heat for 15 minutes. Stir gradually and allow to cool.

To make the brown butter ricotta, add the butter to a shallow pan and cook until it becomes nutty and fragrant. The butter will become brown. Please be mindful as it can burn quickly once it's browned.

Pour the butter over the ricotta, add the salt, heavy cream and lemon zest. Stir until fully incorporated.

Toast your sourdough in a skillet on both sides. Spread the ricotta and add the candied tomato.

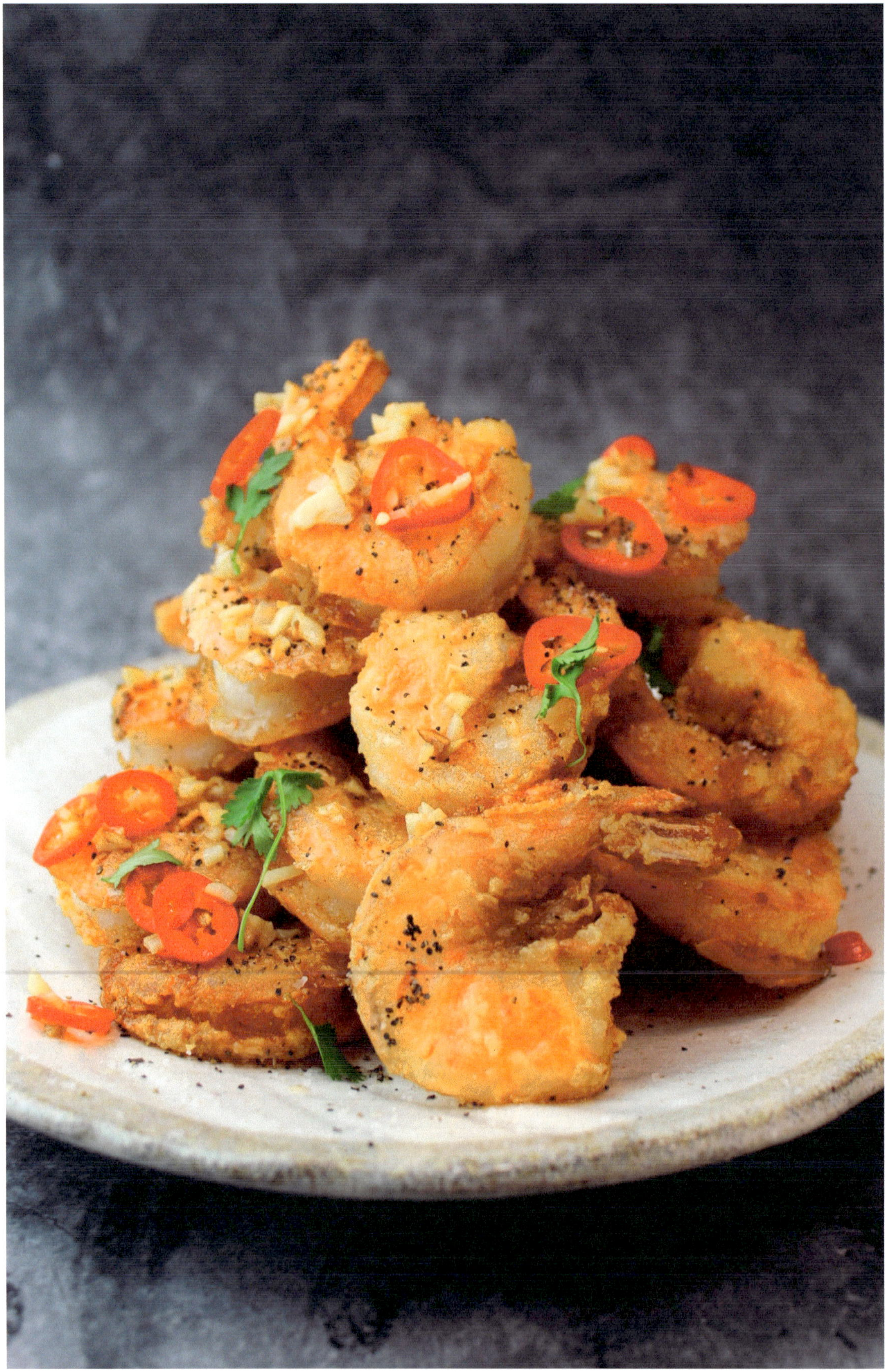

# Salt & Pepper Shrimp

*Serves:* 2-3   *Prep time:* 3 min   *Total time:* 20 min

**Shrimp**
1 cup vegetable oil (for frying)
2 lb extra large shrimp (deveined)
½ cup cornstarch
1 ½ tbsp kosher salt
1 ½ tbsp coarse ground pepper

**Fresno mix**
½ fresno pepper
1 tbsp minced garlic
1 tbsp mirin
1 tbsp rice wine vinegar

Wash and strain your shrimp.

Using a wide rimmed pan, toast the salt and pepper on a medium heat for 4 minutes. Remove the salt and pepper and reserve to season the shrimp after it's been fried.

Add the oil to the pan and bring to a medium heat.

Once the oil is heated, fry the garlic for 20 seconds and place the garlic in the fresno mix.

Coat your shrimp with the cornstarch and shake the excess off prior to frying.

Cook the shrimp for 2 minutes on each side.

Place the shrimp on a baking rack and allow excess oil to drain, this allows the shrimp to remain crisp until you are finished cooking it all.

Place the shrimp in a bowl and toss with the salt and pepper.

Plate the shrimp and pour the fresno garlic mix on top and enjoy immediately.

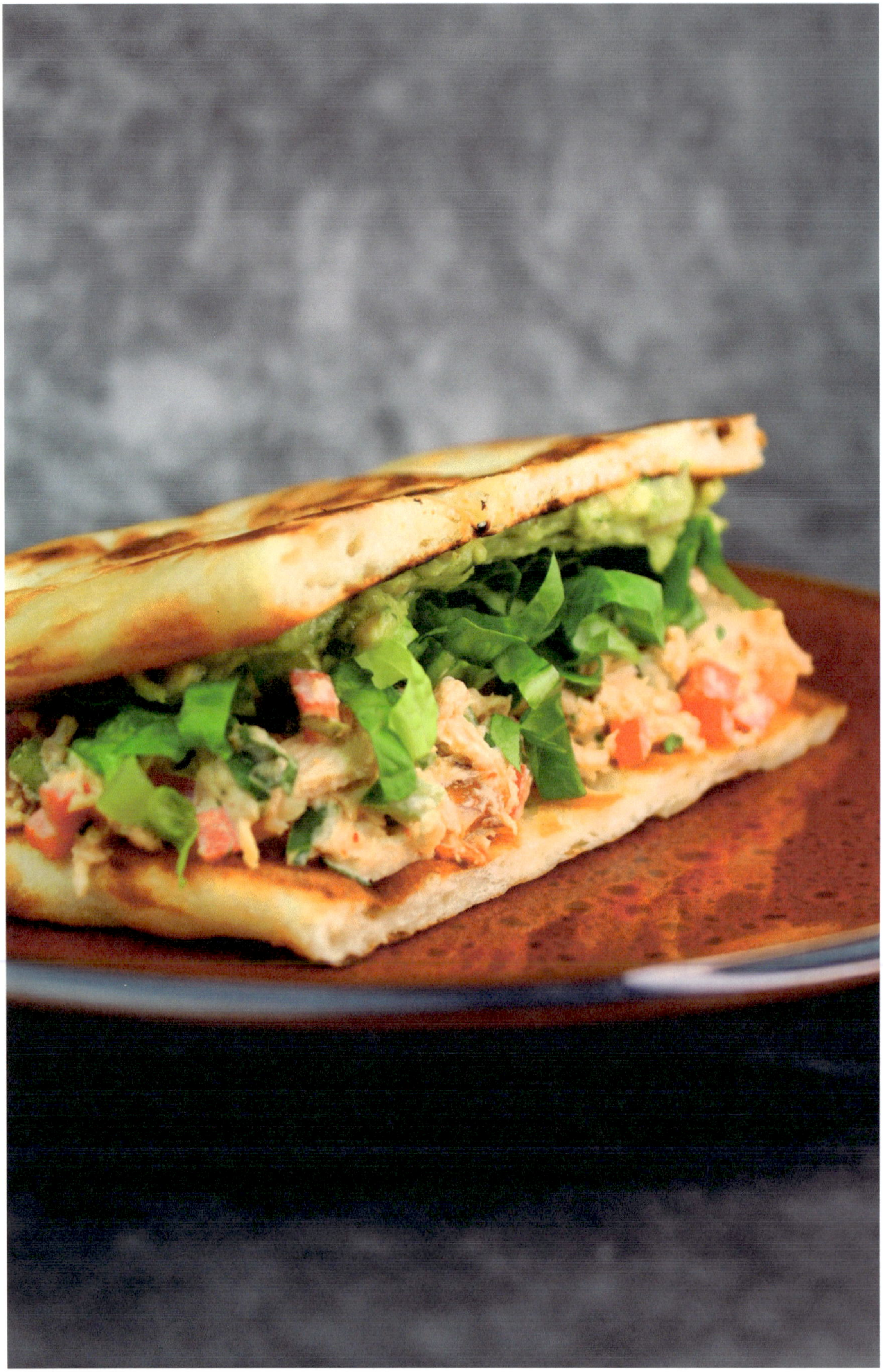

# Chipotle Tunacado

**Serves:** 2   **Prep time:** 10 min   **Total time:** 25 min

**Tuna**
3 tbsp red pepper finely chopped
3 tbsp green pepper finely chopped
1 tbsp celery finely chopped
1 tbsp red onion
1 tbsp minced cilantro
3 tbsp mayo
2 tbsp dijon mustard
1 ½ tbsp chipotle paste
1 tsp kosher salt
1 ½ tsp oregano
1 can of tuna

**Perfect guac**
1 avocado
Juice of ½ lime
1 tsp kosher salt
1 tbsp finely chopped jalapeno pepper
1 ½ tsp finely chopped cilantro
2 Romaine leaves (thinly cut)
Naan Bread

Remove any excess liquid from the tuna prior to adding to the bowl with the chipotle pepper, oregano, salt, mayo, cilantro, red onion, celery, red and green peppers.

For the guac, add all ingredients and mash like there is no tomorrow. I prefer a smooth consistency.

TIP: The naan can be found in the freezer section of a well versed supermarket.

Toast in your oven at 400 degrees for 5 minutes or longer to your liking. Allow to cool, spread the tuna on one half and spread the guac on the other half. Place your shredded lettuce between the two layers and enjoy.

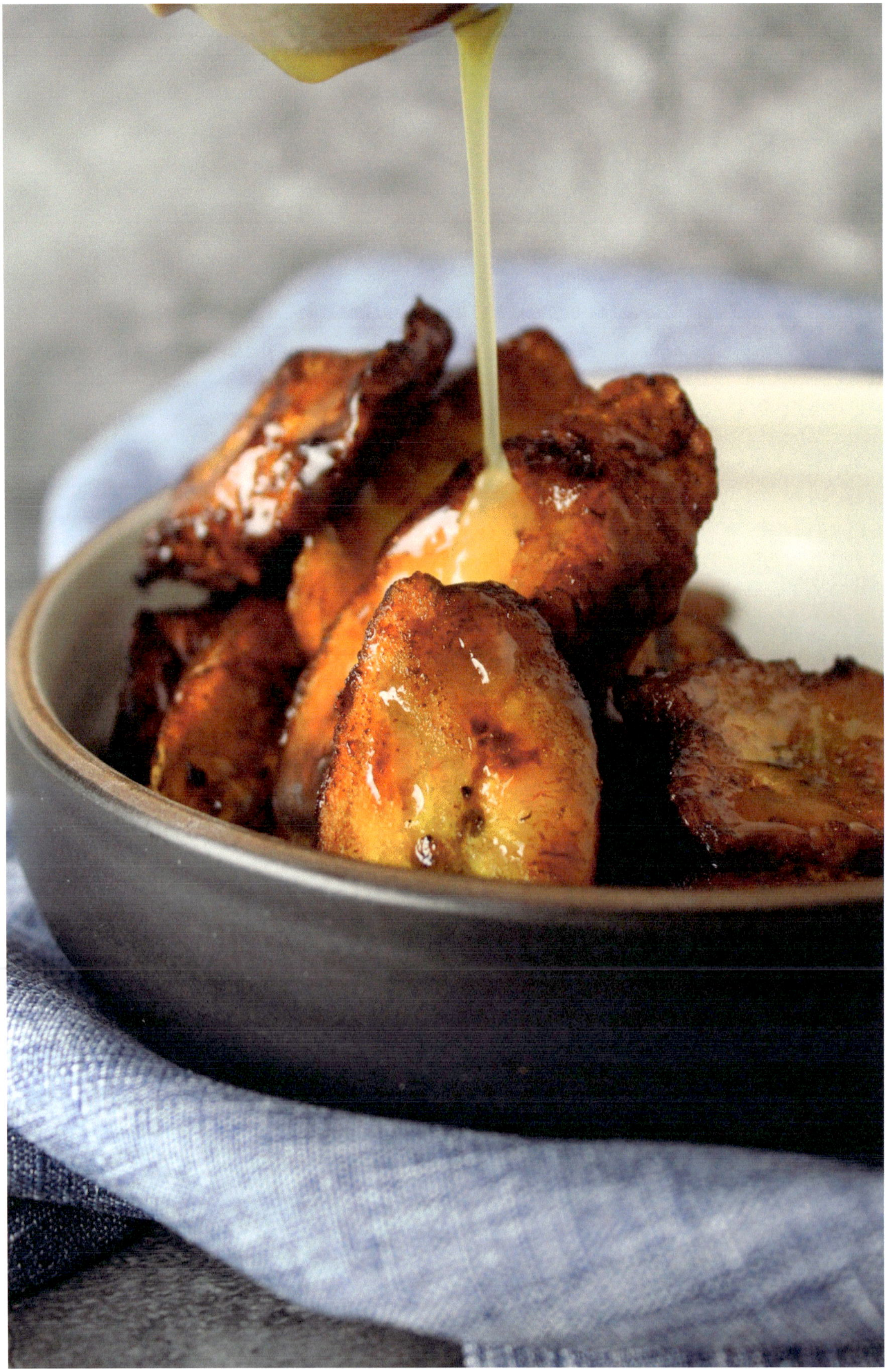

# Sweet Plantain w/ Rum Glaze

*Serves:* 2　　*Prep time:* 10 min　　*Total time:* 15 min

**Plantain**
Vegetable oil for frying
2 ripe sweet plantains

**Rum Glaze**
3 tbsp powdered sugar
1 tbsp butter
1 tsp heavy cream
1 tsp rum

Cut the plantain, ½ inch cuts on a bias.

Using a shallow pan add the vegetable oil, it should be enough to cover the plantains. Cook until a golden brown color is achieved, flip to the other side and do the same.

To make the rum glaze, add all ingredients to a small saucepan and stir on a low heat until fully combined for 2 minutes.

Toss the plantain with the rum glaze and enjoy.

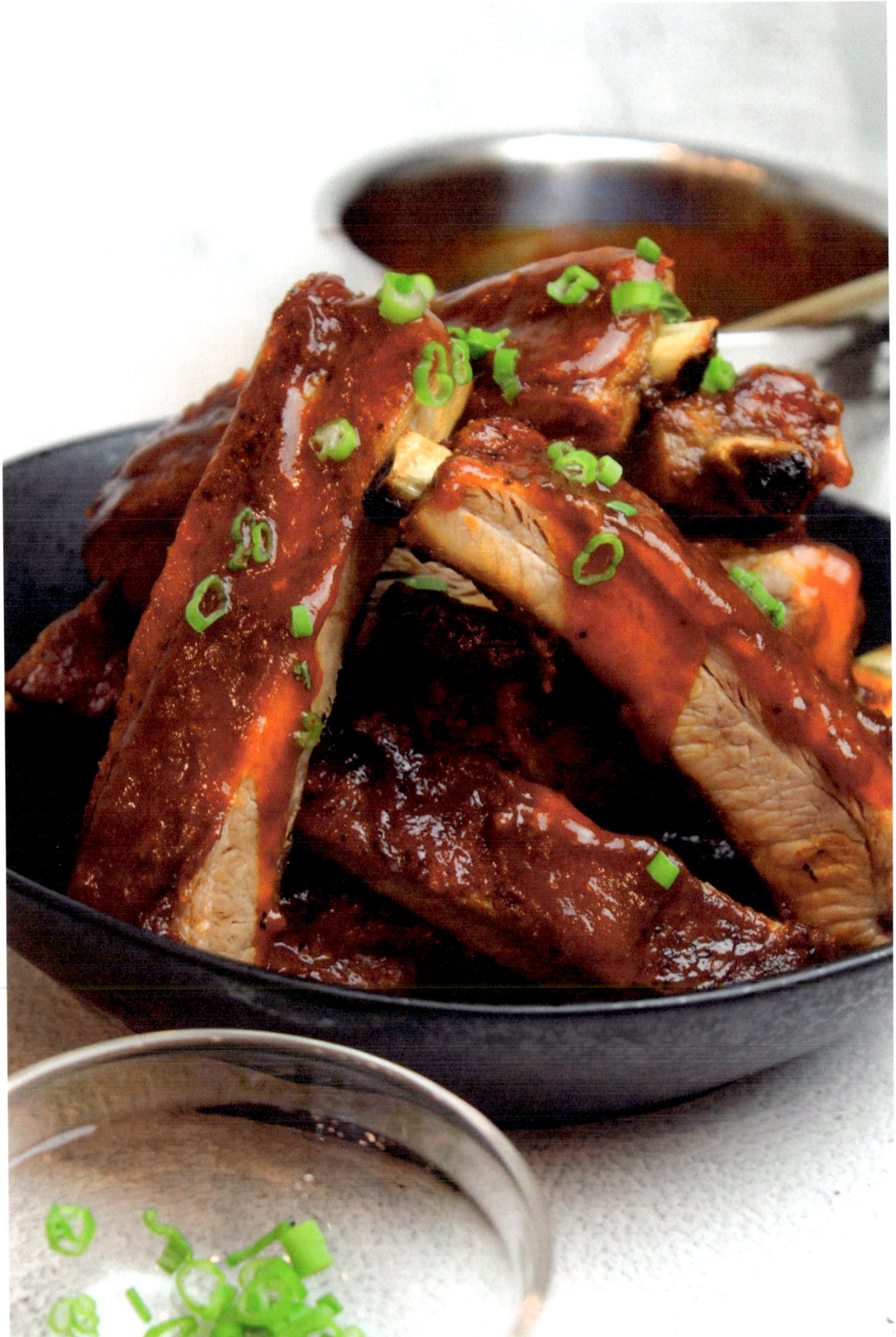

# Henrietta's Ribs

*Serves:* 2-3   *Prep time:* 25 min   *Total time:* 2:45 hr

**Ribs**
1 rack of ribs
3 tbsp dijon mustard

**Dry Rub**
1 tbsp kosher salt
1 tsp paprika
½ tsp cinnamon
1 tsp granulated garlic
1 tsp coarse black pepper
1 tsp white sugar
1 tsp brown sugar

**Sauce**
1 tbsp rice wine vinegar
1 tbsp garlic paste
1 tbsp of sambal
1 tbsp finely minced ginger
¾ cup of your favorite BBQ sauce
3 tbsp of pancake syrup
4 tbsp water
1 ½ tsp dijon mustard
1 tbsp low sodium soy sauce

Garnish with scallion

Remove the membrane from the back end of the ribs.

Rub the dijon mustard on the front and back of the ribs and season the front and back with the mixed dry rub. Press the rub into the dijon.

Place foil on a sheet pan, fully covering and place a wire rack on it. Place the rack flesh side up and into the oven, uncovered for 2 hrs at 325 degrees.

Pour off the excess oil, into a bowl and set aside to easily discard.

Mix all ingredients for the sauce and simmer for 10 minutes on low heat.

Flip the ribs and glaze with the sauce, place them back into the oven for 20 minutes so the glaze can caramelize. Flip and repeat, flesh side up for 20 minutes.

Allow to cool slightly before handling.

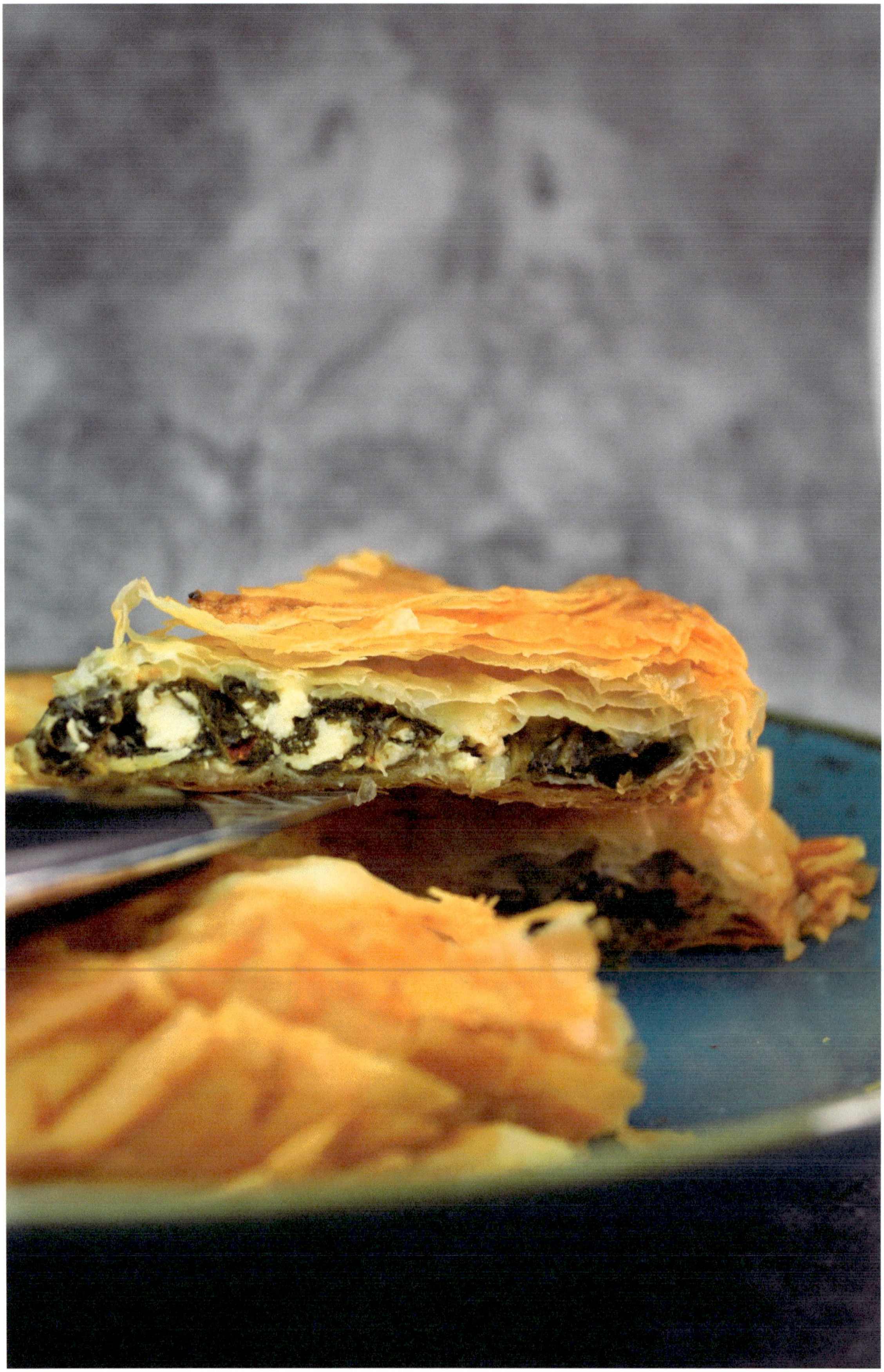

# Spanakopita Pie

*Serves:* 6    *Prep time:* 15 min    Total time: 1 hr

---

**Filling**
1 bag of 6 oz spinach
1 tbsp garlic paste
1 tsp red pepper flakes
1 tsp lemon pepper
1 tbsp granulated garlic
4 oz feta Cheese
1 tbsp olive oil

**Crust**
16 sheets phyllo dough
3 tbsp butter

Heat a saute pan and add the olive oil, spinach, garlic paste, granulated garlic, red pepper flakes until the spinach is completely sweated.

Allow to cool and squeeze out the excess moisture. Fold in the feta cheese.

Preheat your oven to 375 degrees.

Melt the butter and lightly grease the base of your baking dish before adding the first layer of phyllo dough.

Be sure to criss cross the phyllo dough and butter every other layer,

Add your filling and, fold the top layers into the bottom layers to sea. Be sure butter gets onto those edges.

Bake for 30 minutes, the pie will be crispy, allow to cool for 10-15 minutes and enjoy.

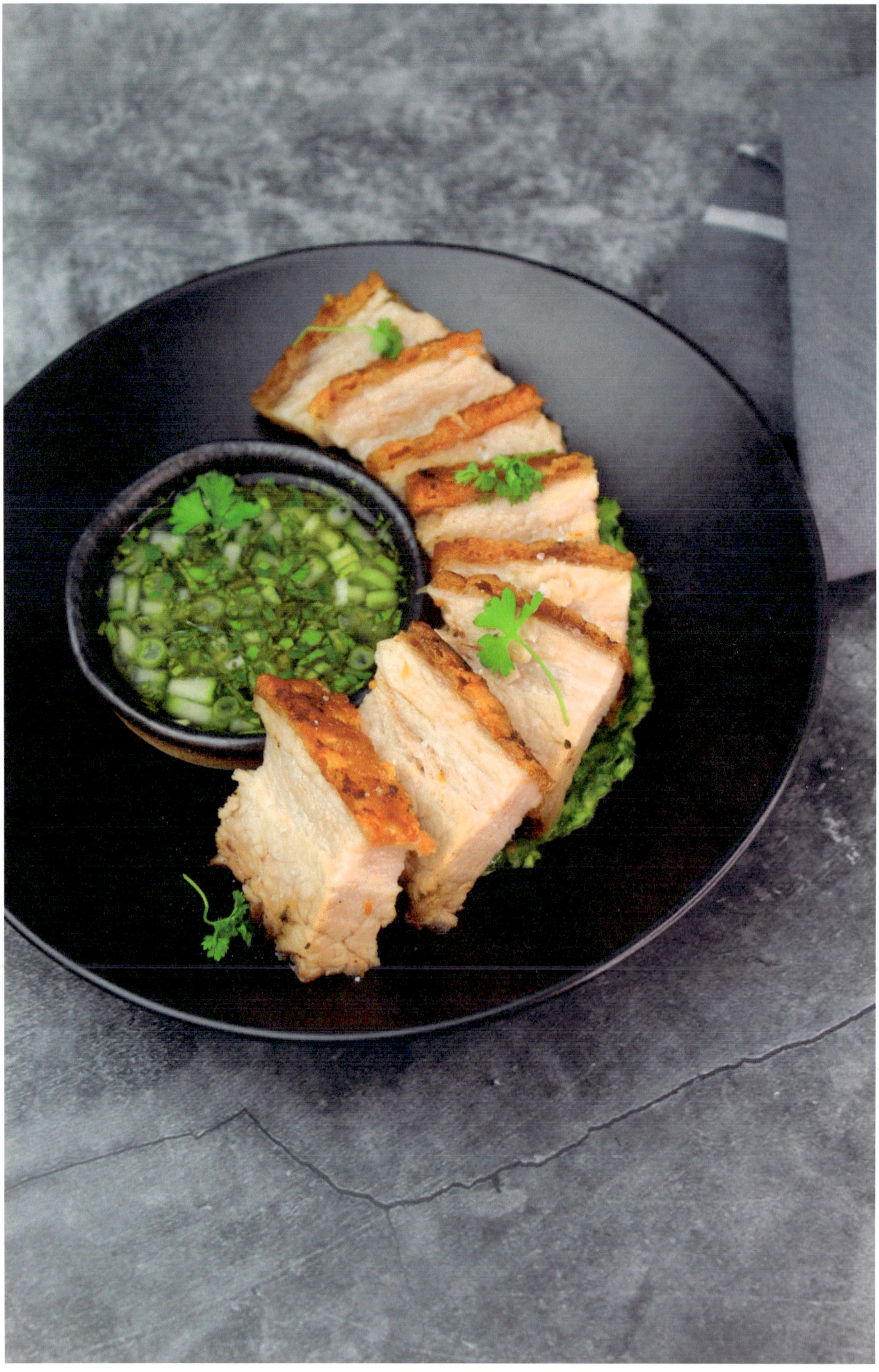

# Saturday Morning Pork Belly

*Serves:* 4  *Prep time:* 15 min  *Total time:* 1 Day

---

**Pork Belly**
1 lb pork belly
1 tsp kosher salt
1 tbsp granulated garlic
1 tsp cinnamon
1 tsp paprika
1 tbsp paprika
2 tbsp green seasoning
vinegar(for brushing the fat)

**Green Seasoning**
1 bulb of garlic
1 cup culantro
Scallion 2 bunches
1 scotch bonnet
1 cup parsley
1 tbsp thyme rough chopped
4 tbsp olive oil
1 tbsp salt

**Souse juice**
1 lime
1 cup cucumber
⅓ cup of scallion
½ scotch bonnet finely cut
1 tbsp finely chopped parsley
1 ½ tbsp salt
1 tbsp sugar

To make your green seasoning, add the garlic, culantro, scallion, scotch bonnet, parsley, thyme, olive oil and salt to a food processor and blend until you have fine chunks.

Be sure to pat dry your pork, make ¼ inch slits in the skin (try not to break the fat)

Flip the pork belly over and make 1 inch slits across the flesh, season with the salt, granulated garlic, cinnamon, paprika and green seasoning, rubbing into the crevices of the meat. Be sure not to get the seasoning onto the skin.

With the skin side up, let the pork belly air dry on the bottom shelf of your fridge for 24hrs.

Preheat your oven to 370 degrees, Get a large piece of foil and create a rectangle around the pork, be sure to crimp the edges.

Cook for 60 minutes.

Remove from the heat and brush with 1 tbsp of vinegar and sprinkle a bit of kosher salt. Place into the oven with the broiler on for 35 minutes.

Make your souse by squeezing the juice of 1 lime, the cup of water and adding the cucumber, scallion, scotch bonnet, parsley and sugar. This must be prepared as the pork is cooking for freshness.

Once the pork is cooked, allow it to rest for 15 minutes before slicing. Add some of the green seasoning to the base of your plate, add the pork belly on top and serve with the souse juice.

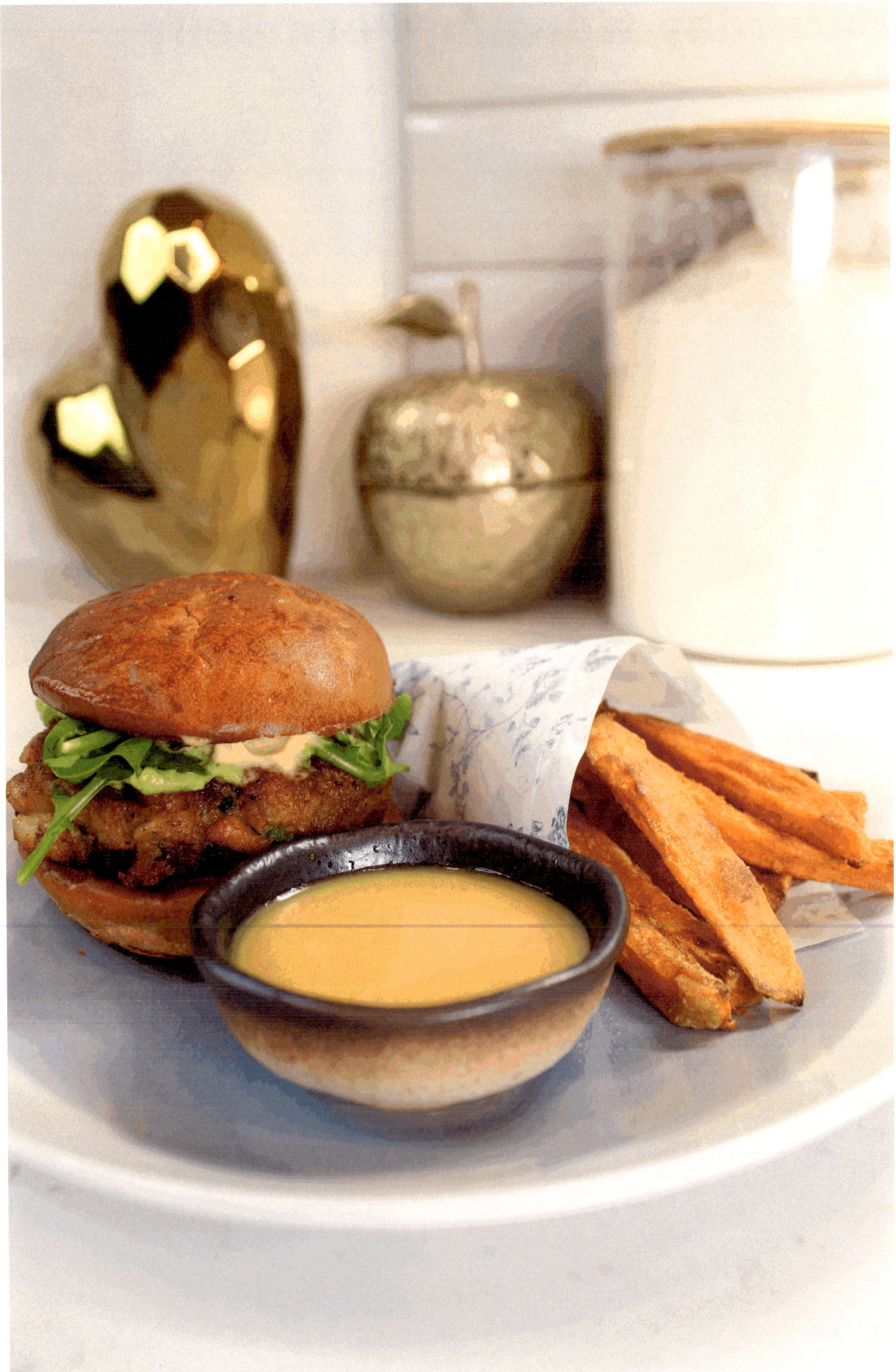

# Shrimp Burger

***Serves:*** *8*     ***Prep time:*** *15 min*     ***Total time:*** *1 hr*

---

**Shrimp Patty**
2 lbs of shrimp
1 ½ tbsp cilantro rough chopped
½ cup panko
1 egg
1 tsp red pepper flakes
1 tbsp minced ginger
1 tbsp minced garlic
½ cup scallion thin sliced
1 tsp soy sauce
1 tsp sesame oil
1 tsp curry powder
1 tsp herb de provence
1 tsp garlic powder
1 tsp old bay
⅛ tsp clove
⅛ tsp allspice
½ tsp sugar
½ cumin
⅛ cinnamon

**Avocado crema**
2 avocados
¼ medium onion
½ jalapeno
Juice of 1 lime
1 tsp kosher salt
1 tbsp minced cilantro
1 cup sour cream

**Peppa Sauce Mayo**
**1** cup mayo
2 tbsp pepper sauce

**Sweet potato fries**
2 sweet potatoes
1 tbsp cornstarch
1 tsp kosher salt
½ tsp cumin
2 tbsp olive oil

Place the shrimp in a food processor and pulse. While we want to ground the shrimp, we still want chunks.

Add the shrimp, egg, sesame oil, soy sauce, garlic, ginger, scallion, cilantro and spices to a bowl and mix, then add the panko.

Form 8 patties tightly, place on a sheet pan and refrigerate for 15 minutes.

Preheat the oven to 375 degrees. Cut the sweet potato into ½ inch strips and coat with the cornstarch and spices. Spread on a sheet pan and bake for 30 minutes. Give the sweet potato a toss on the sheet pan at the 15 minute mark.

For the avocado crema, add all ingredients to a blender and blend until fully smooth.

Mix the mayo and pepper sauce and refrigerate.

Heat a pan with oil and sea for 3 minutes on each side.

Toast your buns, place the cooked shrimp patty down, avocado crema, arugula and peppa sauce mayo

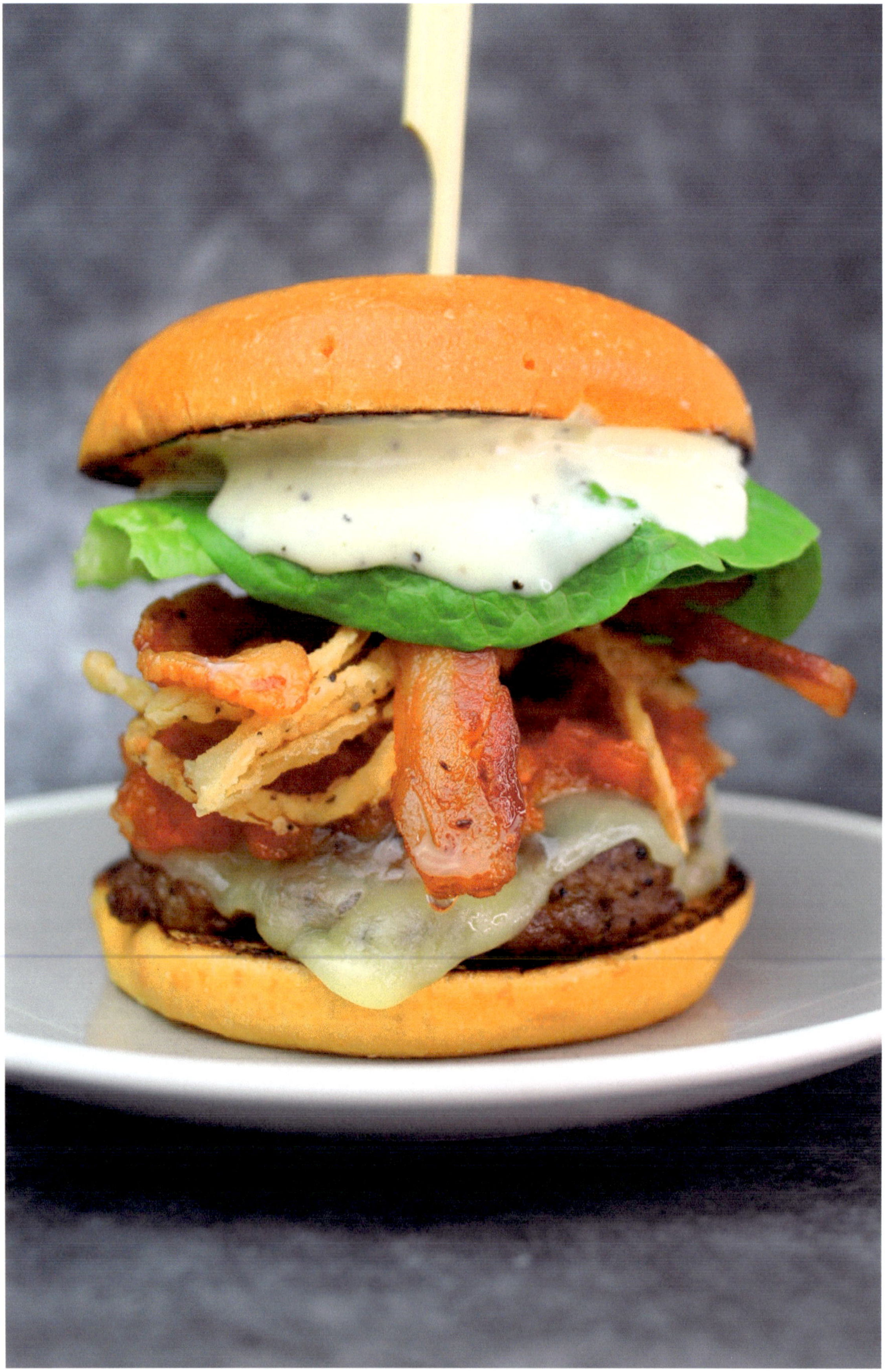

# The Brooklyn Burger

*Serves:* 8       *Prep time:* 25 min       *Total time:* 1 hr

---

**Tomato jam**
3 roma tomato deseeded
1 small onion
5 tbsp sugar
1 tbsp vinegar
1 tsp salt
½ fresno pepper

**Bacon**
Let's be real! Add as much bacon as you want!

**Onion Rings**
2 onions thinly sliced
1 cup flour
1 tbsp sugar
1 tsp pepper
1 ½ tsp salt

**Garlic Aioli**
4 cloves of garlic
Zest of 1 lemon
1 tsp crack pepper
1 tbsp dijon mustard
3 egg yolk
1 ¼ cup olive oil
Juice of 1 lemon
1 tsp salt

**Burger**
3 lbs ground beef
½ onion finely chopped
2 tbsp worcestershire sauce
1 tbsp garlic
1 tbsp kosher salt
1 tbsp coarse ground pepper
1 tbsp italian seasoning

Romaine lettuce
Brioche buns
Cheddar cheese

Add all the ingredients for the tomato jam into the food processor and pulse, leaving some texture. Add to a pot and cook on a medium heat for 25 minutes.

Preheat the oven to 400 degrees and cook the bacon for 20 minutes, until fully cooked.

Mix the ground beef, onion, worcestershire sauce, garlic, kosher salt, pepper and italian seasoning. Form 8 burgers, refrigerate for 20 minutes.

Take the thinly sliced onions and place in ice cold water for 15 minutes.

For the garlic aioli, add all ingredients to a blender and combine, slowly add the oil to emulsify.

Heat a pot of frying oil. Strain the onions and toss in a bowl with the flour, sugar and pepper.

Shake off the excess flour and fry the onions for 30 seconds. Once removed from the oil, leave space between the onion rings so they don't sweat.

Cook the burgers on a flat top for 6 - 7 minutes on each side, add the cheese as the burger is finishing.

Toast your buns lightly and assemble with as many toppings as you prefer and enjoy.

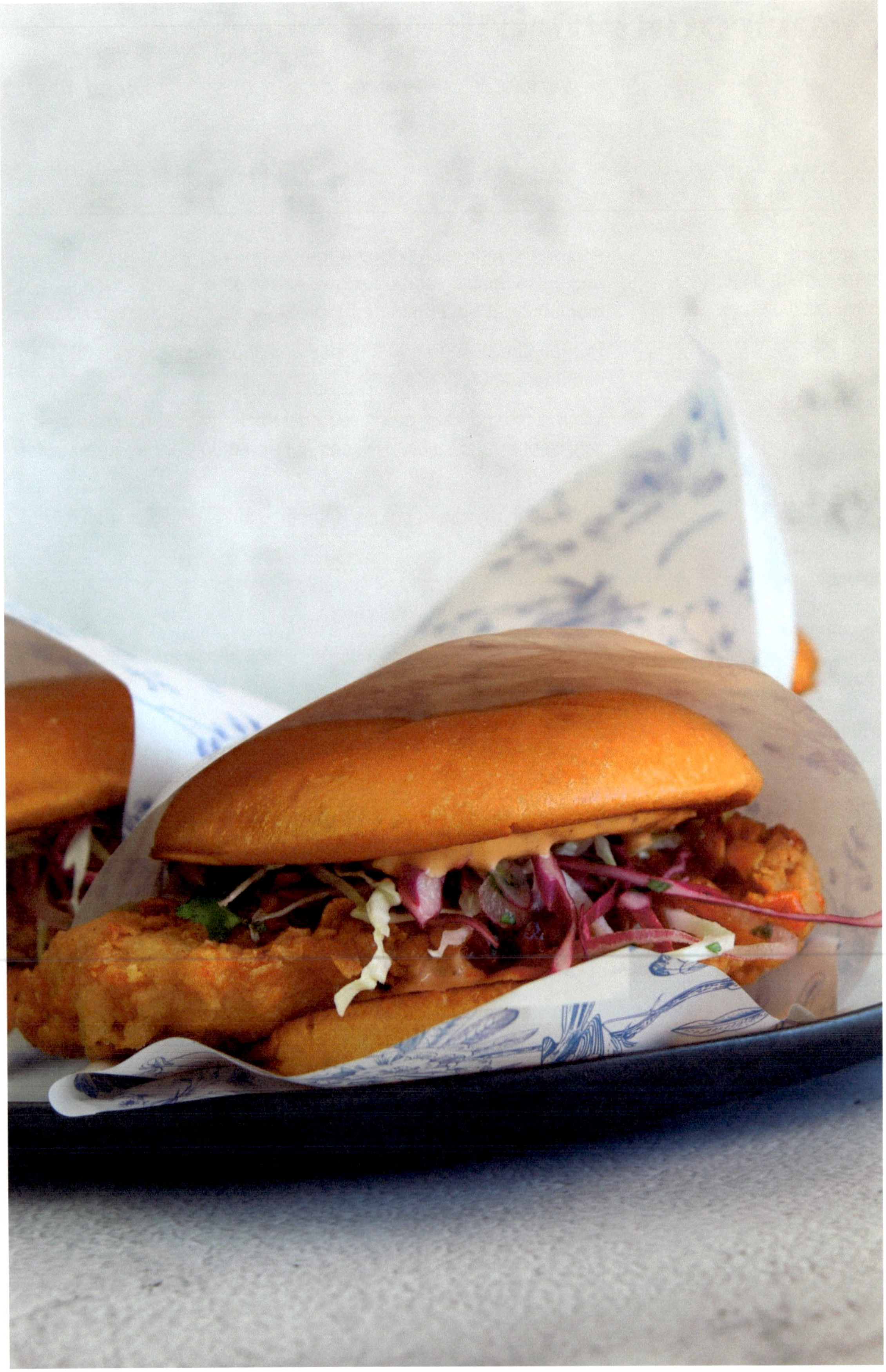

# Infamous Fried Chicken Sando

*Serves:* 6     *Prep time:* 45 min     Total  time: *1 hr*

---

**Chicken**
3 chicken breasts
1 tsp paprika
1 tbsp garlic powder
1 tsp kosher salt
1 tsp lemon pepper
1 tbsp hot sauce
1 cup of buttermilk

**Flour Dredge**
1 cup flour
½ cup cornstarch
1 tsp kosher salt
1 tsp paprika
1 tsp garlic powder

**Slaw**
¼ red cabbage thinly sliced
¼ cup green cabbage thinly sliced
¼ red onion thinly sliced
1 tbsp of cilantro roughly chopped
1 tbsp rice wine vinegar
1 tsp sugar

**Chipotle Mayo**
1 cup mayo
1 tbsp chipotle paste

**The Glaze**
1 tbsp gochujang
4 tbsp ketchup
1 tbsp rice wine vinegar
2 tbsp water
1 tbsp Grand Marnier

Vegetable oil to fry
Brioche buns

Slice the chicken lengthwise into two. You will have 6 pieces total. Using a fork or knife, pierce the chicken and marinate with the hot sauce, paprika, salt, lemon pepper, buttermilk and garlic powder for a minimum of 30 minutes or overnight.

Mix the ingredients for the chipotle mayo together and hold in the fridge.

For the slaw, add all ingredients except the sugar and vinegar. You will do this as you're building the sandwich to maintain the crispness of the lettuce.

Make the glaze by adding the gochujang, ketchup, rice wine vinegar,water and cognac to a pot and heat for 10 minutes to marry those flavors.

Using a large pot or deep dryer, heat your oil to 375 degrees.

In a bowl, mix your flour dredge and add the chicken. Give the chicken a nice toss to coat fully, be sure to squeeze the flour onto the chicken and shake off the excess flour.

Carefully place the chicken in the oil and fry for 8 minutes.

Place your cooked chicken on a baking rack and allow it to cool slightly before handling.

Toast your buns, place  the chicken down & glaze, toss the slaw together and place on top of the chicken. Add chipotle mayo on the top bun  and enjoy the most delectable sandwich.

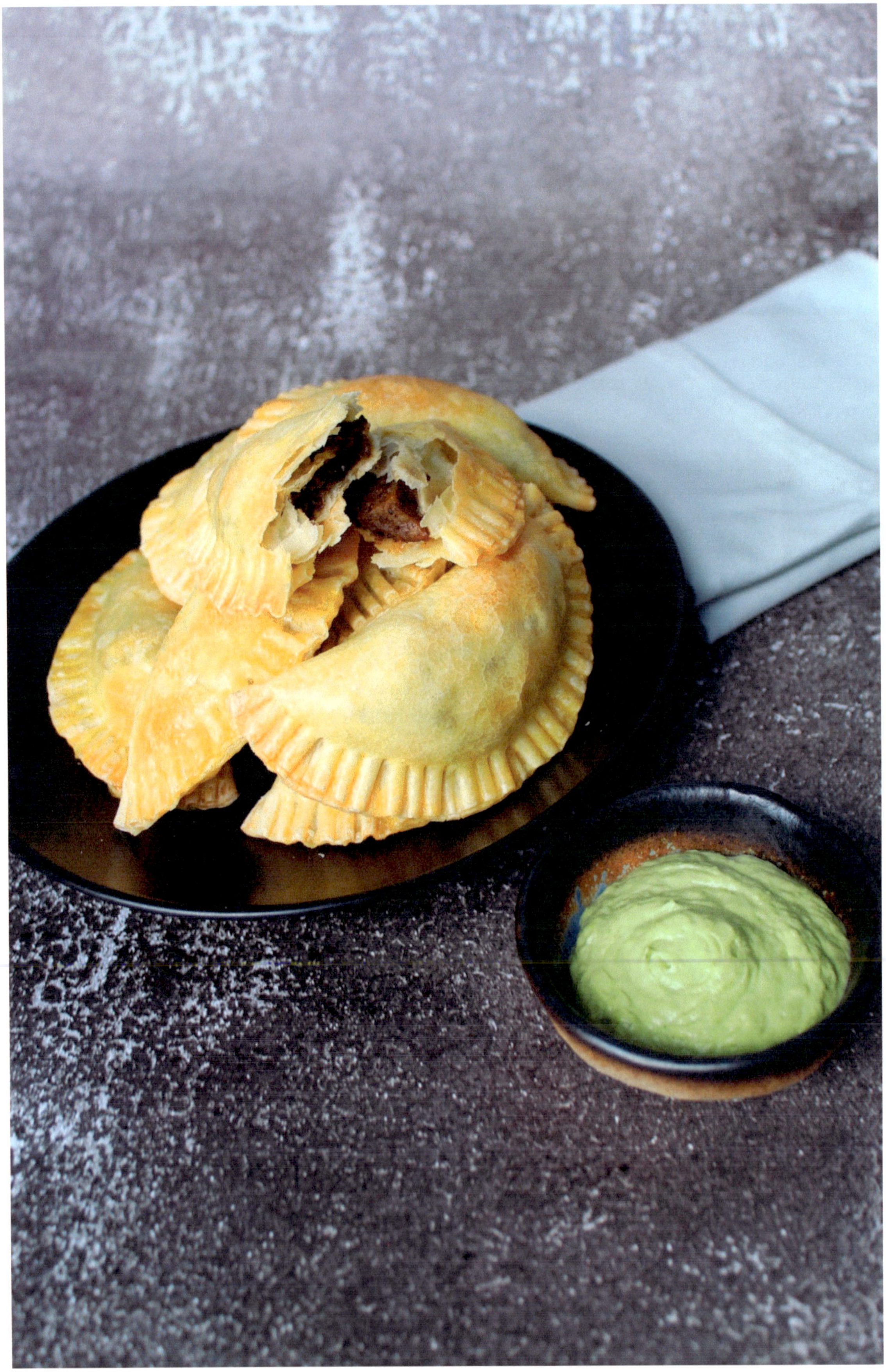

# Jerk Mushroom Empanadas

***Serves:*** *6*  ***Prep time:*** *1 hr*  ***Total time:*** *1 hr*

**Filling**
1 sweet plantain
1 pack crimini mushrooms
½ onion finely diced
5 cloves of garlic finely chopped
1 tbsp finely chopped thyme
1 tbsp granulated garlic
⅛ tsp allspice
⅛ tsp clove
⅛ tsp cinnamon
1 tbsp low sodium soy sauce
1 tbsp jerk seasoning
1 tsp salt (reserve until the mushrooms are cooked through)
2 tbsp olive oil

Vegetable oil to fry plantain
Baking empanada disc (found in the frozen section

**Egg wash**
1 egg beaten
1 ½ tbsp water

Cut the plantain into small cubes 1/3 of an inch and fry until golden brown for 30 seconds.

Using a food processor, pulse the mushrooms to get small bits, you're looking for pieces that will be a bit smaller than pea size.

Add 2 tbsp of oil to a saute pan, on medium heat, add the aromatics of the onion, garlic and thyme. Add the mushrooms and all spices except salt. Saute for 10 minutes, add the soy sauce and salt, cook for an additional 5 minutes.

Mix with the cooked plantain and allow to cool.

Using thawed empanada discs, add your filling, be sure to leave room to properly close the empanadas. To do so, you will fold the empanada disc in half and crimp the edges tightly with a fork.

Place on a parchment lined baking pan, brush with egg wash and bake for 25 minutes (please follow the instructions of the brand you have purchased.)

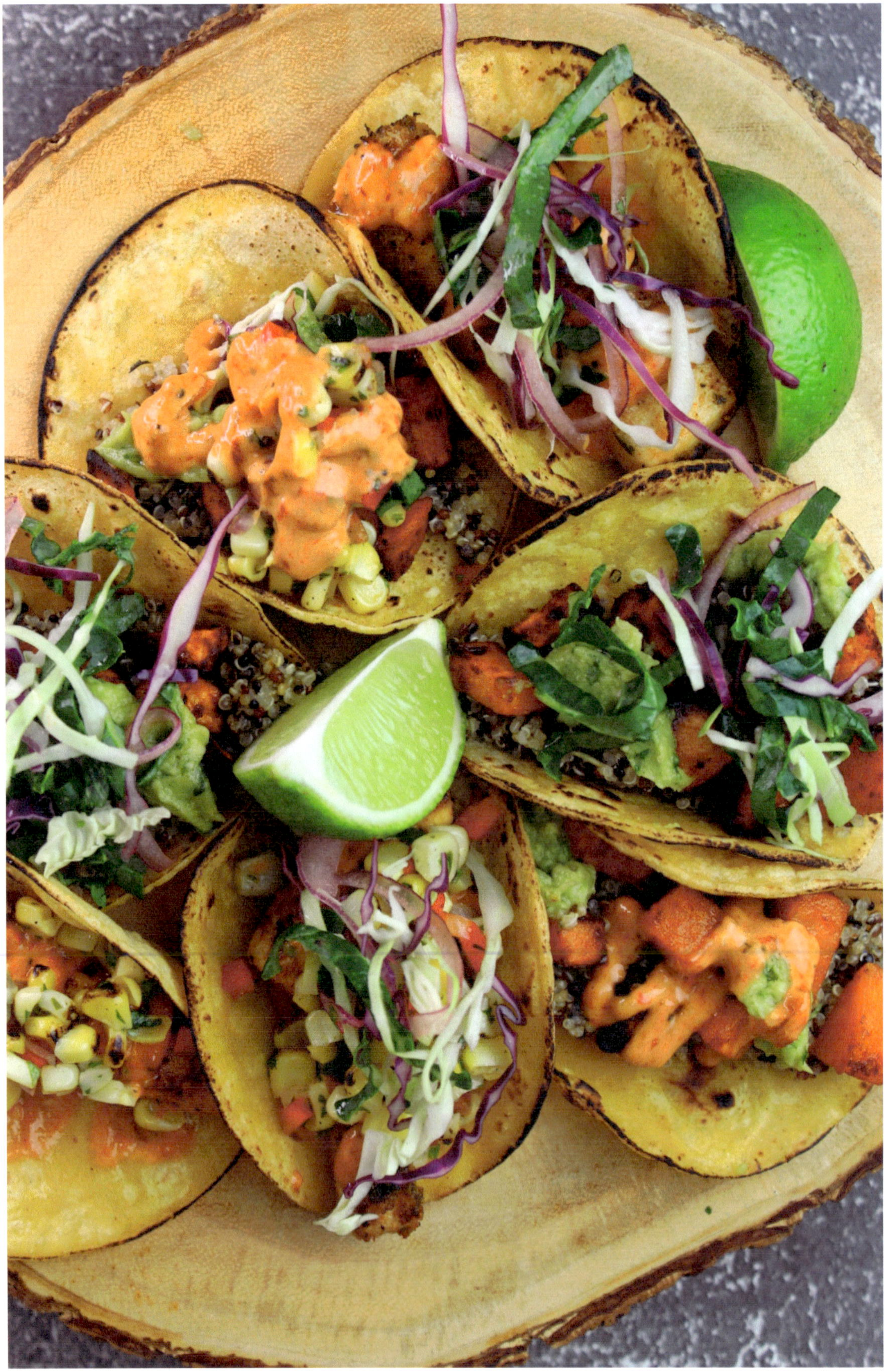

# Sweet Potato Quinoa Tacos

*Serves:* 2    *Prep time:* 1 hr    *Total time:* 1 hr

---

2 cups sweet potato diced ½ inch cuts
1 tbsp chipotle paste
2 tbsp olive oil
1 tsp paprika
1 tsp minced garlic
1 tsp sugar
1 tsp salt

**Quinoa**
½ cup quinoa
1 cup of water
1 ½ tsp olive oil
1 tsp oregano
1 tsp salt
1 ½ tsp finely minced cilantro

**Slaw**
¼ red cabbage thinly sliced
¼ cup green cabbage thinly sliced
¼ red onion thinly sliced
1 tbsp of cilantro roughly chopped
1 tbsp rice wine vinegar
1 tsp sugar

**Perfect guac**
1 avocado
Juice of ½ lime
1 tsp kosher salt
1 tbsp finely chopped jalapeno pepper
1 ½ tsp finely chopped cilantro

Preheat your oven to 350 degrees.

Toss the sweet potato, olive oil, chipotle paste, garlic, paprika, salt and sugar together and put on a baking pan. Bake for 25 minutes, until tender.

Add the quinoa and water to a pot and cook for 15 mins. Once finished, add the olive oil, oregano, salt, cilantro and mix well.

Make your guac by adding all ingredients to a bowl and mash until you get the texture you prefer.

For the slaw, add all ingredients except the sugar and vinegar. You will do this as you're building the tacos to maintain the crispness of the lettuce.

Lightly saute both sides of the tortillas with a bit of oil. Stack and wrap in a moist paper towel to retain moisture.

Build the tacos, add the sweet potato, quinoa, guac & slaw.

# Swordfish Tacos

**Serves:** 2  **Prep time:** 1 hr  **Total time:** 1 hr

---

**Swordfish**
1 lb of swordfish
1 /2 tsp salt
Juice of ½ lime
2 cups of water
1 tbsp green seasoning **(See Page )**
1 tsp paprika
1 tsp lemon pepper
1 tsp garlic powder
1 tsp onion powder
2 tbsp canola oil

**Corn salsa**
1 ear of corn
¼ red pepper minced
½ jalapeno minced
1 tsp cilantro finely chopped
¼ red onion chopped
½ tsp salt
1 tsp olive oil
Juice of ½ lime

**Chipotle lime crema**
1 cup sour cream
1 ½ tbsp fresh lime juice
Zest of half a lime
1 tsp salt
1 tbsp chipotle paste

Slice the swordfish into ½ inch strips and add to a bowl with the water, salt and lime. Allow to soak for 20 minutes.

Rinse the fish, pat dry and season with the green seasoning, paprika, garlic and onion. Marinate for 30 minutes.

Add oil to the pan and cook the fish for 3 minutes on each side.

To make the corn salsa, roast the corn on your stove top with a high open flame for 5 minutes, giving an occasional turn to cook thoroughly. Add the red pepper, jalapeno, cilantro, red onion, lime juice, salt and olive oil. Mix and allow to chill.

Mix all ingredients to create the chipotle lime crema and keep refrigerated until needed.

Lightly saute both sides of the tortillas with a bit of oil. Stack and wrap in a moist paper towel to retain moisture.

Build the tacos, add the corn salsa and chipotle lime crema.

A Fresh Take

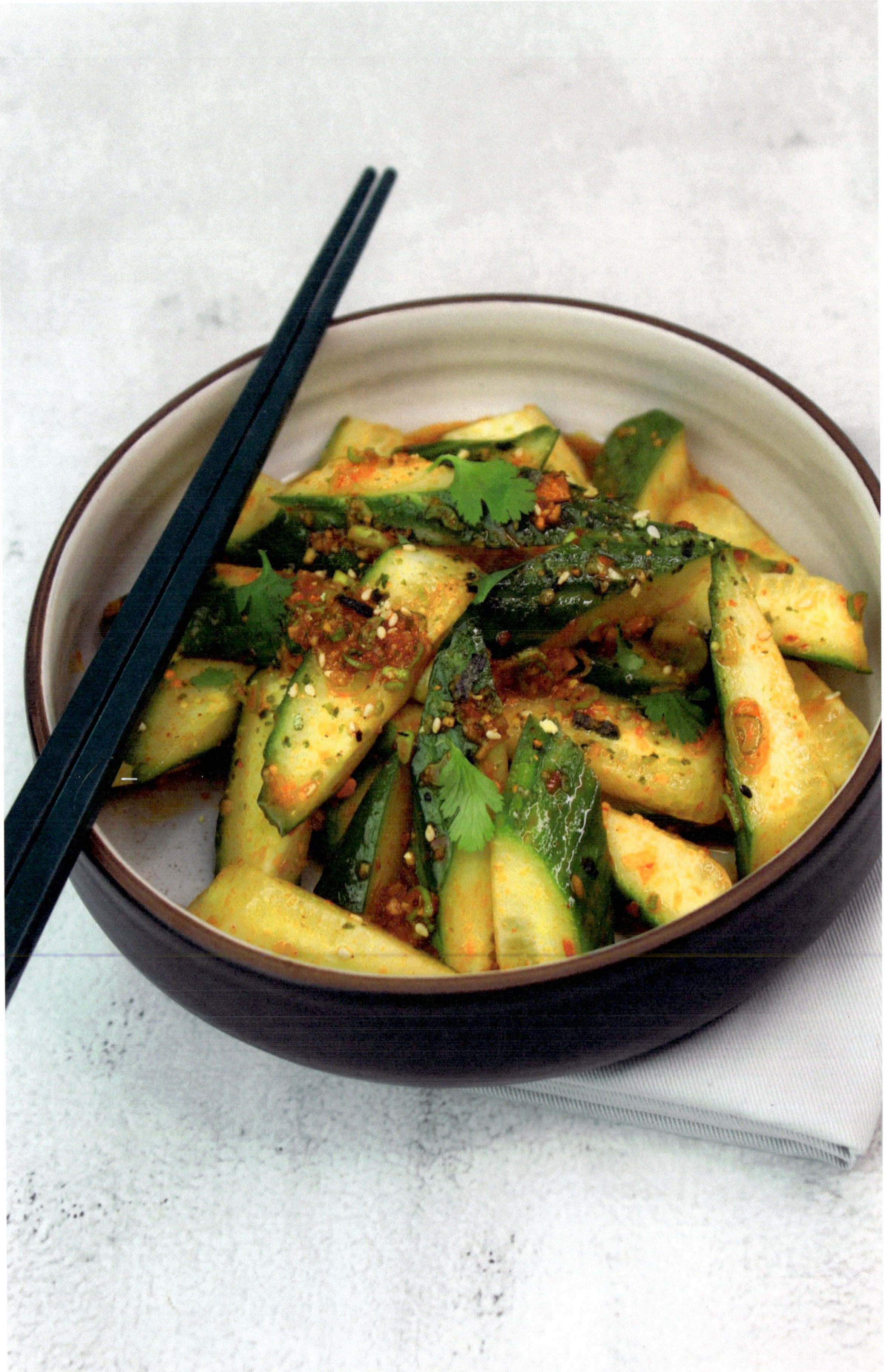

# Cucumber Nosh

*Serves:* 2   *Prep time:* 10 min   *Total time:* 15 min

---

1 cucumber
½ scallion sliced thinly
½ tsp ginger finely minced
½ tsp finely minced garlic
1 tbsp tamari soy sauce
1 tbsp sesame oil
2 tbsp sugar
2 tbsp lime juice
1 tbsp spicy crispy garlic (can be found in your local Asian market)
Furikake dusting

Slice the cucumber in half lengthwise, cut on a bias, against each slice.

Mix all ingredients in except the cucumber and scallions.

Add all ingredients to a bowl and mix.

Top with a small amount of the furikake dusting and enjoy.

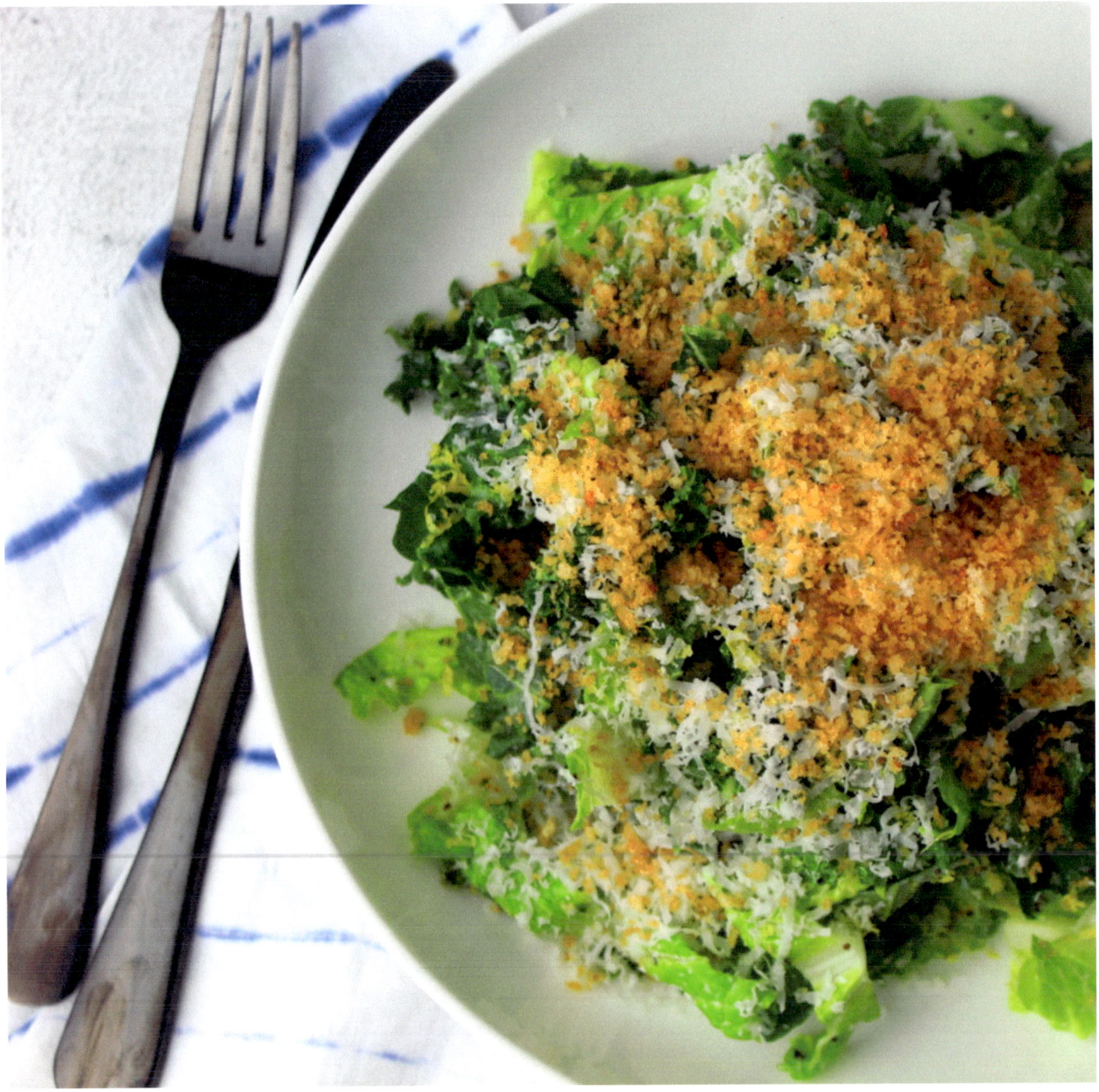

# Spiced Caesar Salad

***Serves:*** *2*  ***Prep time:*** *20 min*  ***Total time:*** *20 min*

---

3 cups romaine
3 cups kale
Zest of half a lemon
1 tsp kosher salt
1 tsp coarse ground pepper
Fresh parmesan

½ cup caesar dressing
Franks Red Hot sauce
⅛ tsp cayenne

**Bread crumbs**
1 cup panko
1 tsp chopped parsley
1 tsp salt
½ tsp Old Bay
1 tsp granulated garlic
½ tsp smoked paprika

Clean the romaine and kale w/ cold heavily salted water to remove debris.

Drain the excess moisture using a salad spinner or paper towel.

In a medium saute pan, add the oil, panko, spices and parsley. Move around the pan so the bread crumbs don't burn. Toast for 4-5 minutes and let cool.

Mix all ingredients for the caesar dressing.

Once the greens are dry, add the salt, pepper, lemon zest, parmesan and the spicy caesar dressing. (As much or as little as little as you prefer.)

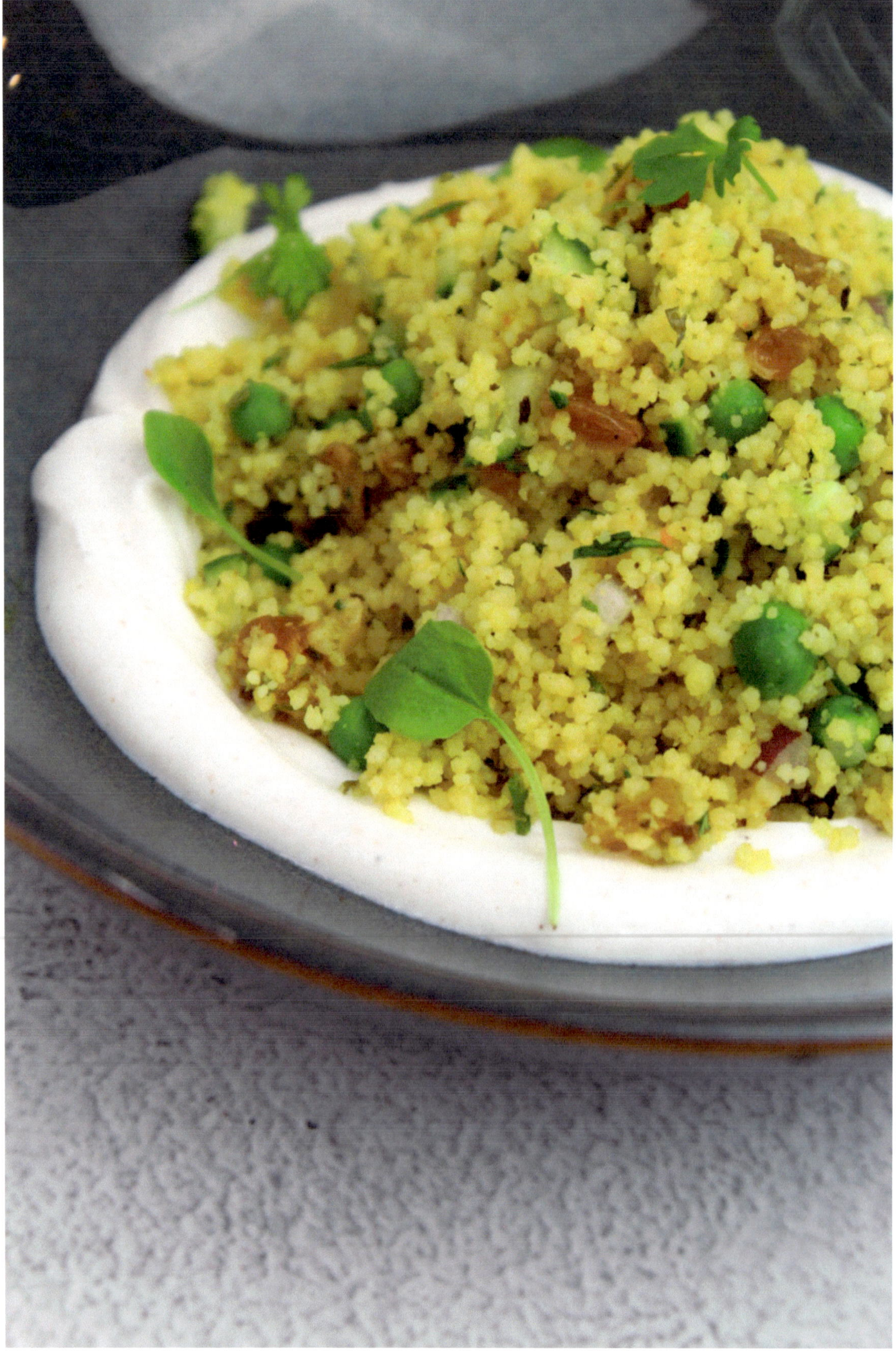

# Couscous Salad

**Serves:** 2    **Prep time:** 1 hr    **Total time:** 1 hr

---

1 pack 5oz couscous
¼ red onion diced small
½ cup raisins
½ cup cucumber deseeded and dice
1 tbsp finely chopped cilantro
½ cup frozen peas
Juice of 1 lime
1 ½ tsp kosher salt
 tbsp curry powder
1 ½ cup steaming water
3 tbsp olive oil

1 cup greek yogurt or vegan crema
⅛ tsp tsp cinnamon
⅛ tsp salt

Place the pack of couscous in a bowl, add the olive oil, curry and salt, stir and add the steaming water. Cover and leave for 15 minutes.

Once the couscous is cooked, fluff and add the red onion, cucumber, cilantro, raisins, peas and stir.

Mix the yogurt, cinnamon and salt.

Place the yogurt on the plate, top with the couscous and enjoy.

This can be served warm or cold.

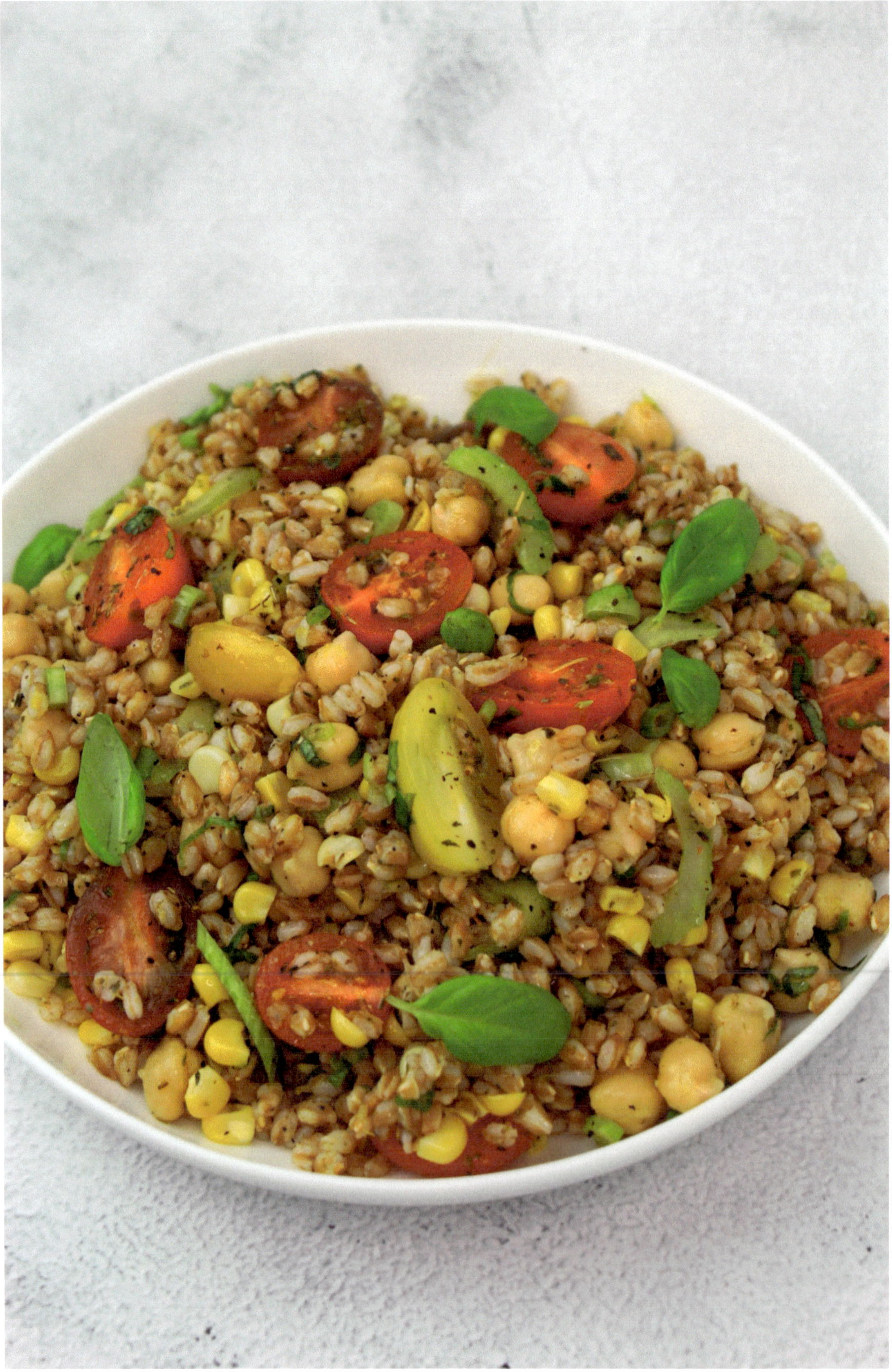

# Farro Summer Salad

**Serves:** 4  **Prep time:** 45 min  **Total time:** 1hr

1 cup farro
2 cups water
1 tsp salt
3 tbsp olive oil
1 ear of corn shaved
1 cup cherry tomatoes sliced
1 stick of celery thin bias cut
1 cup of cooked chickpeas
¼ cup scallions thinly sliced
1 tsp lemon pepper
1 tbsp herb de provence
Juice of ½ a lemon
Zest of ½ lemon
Salt and pepper to taste

Rince the farro, add the water and salt and cook for 20 minutes on a medium heat. Add olive oil, fluff and allow to cool.

Once the farro is cooled, add all of the remaining ingredients and serve cold.

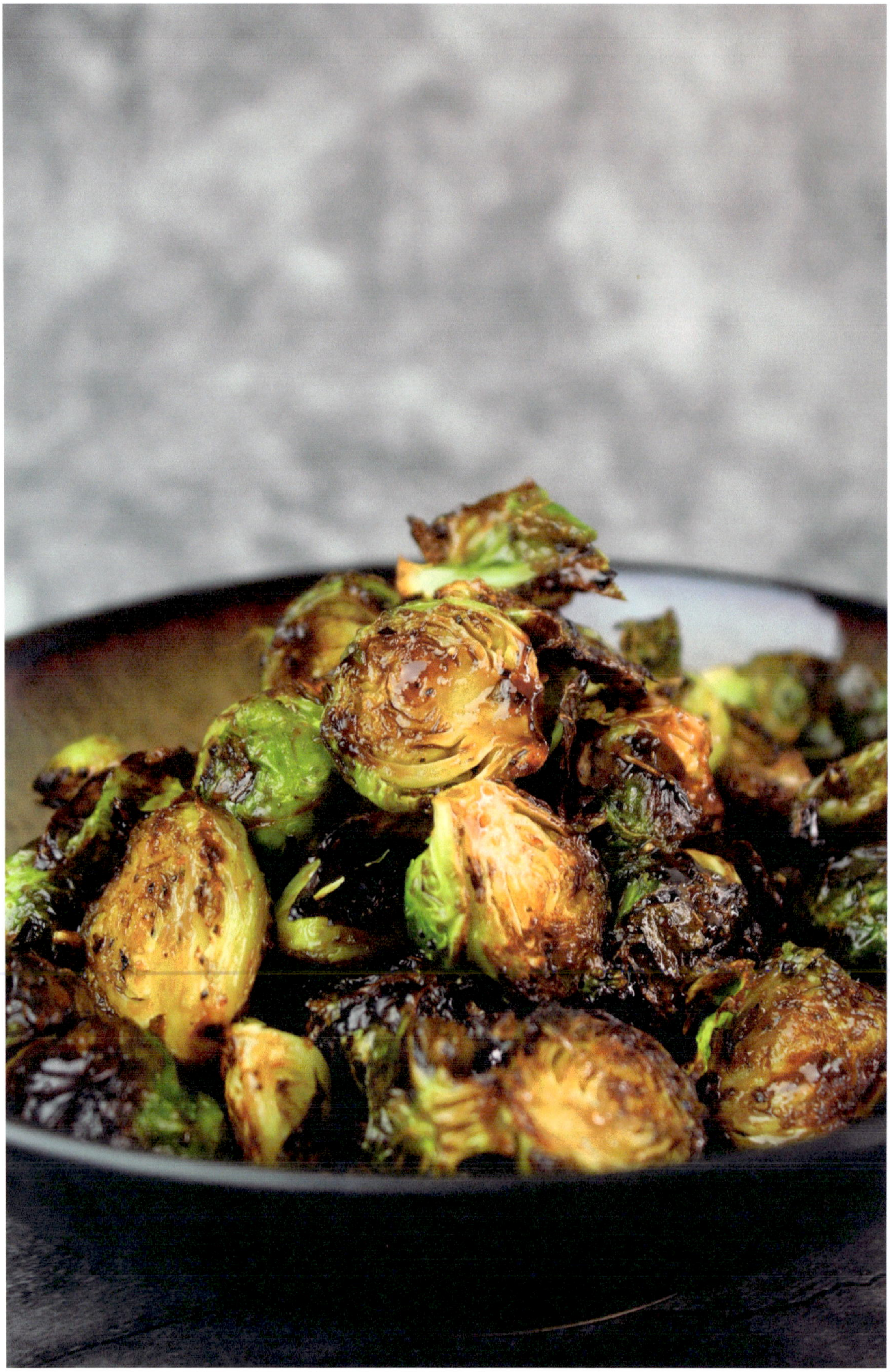

# Crispy Honey Brussel Sprouts

**Serves:** 2   **Prep time:** 5 min   **Total time:** 15 min

---

1 lb brussel sprouts
2 tbsp olive oil
1 tsp salt
1 tsp coarse ground pepper
1 tsp hot honey
1 tbsp balsamic glaze
1 tsp garlic paste

Trim the brussel sprouts and cut in half, add the salt, olive oil and pepper to coat and place in the air fryer at 400 degrees for 10 minutes.

In a bowl, mix the balsamic glaze, honey and garlic. Once the brussel sprouts are finished, toss in the glaze and enjoy.

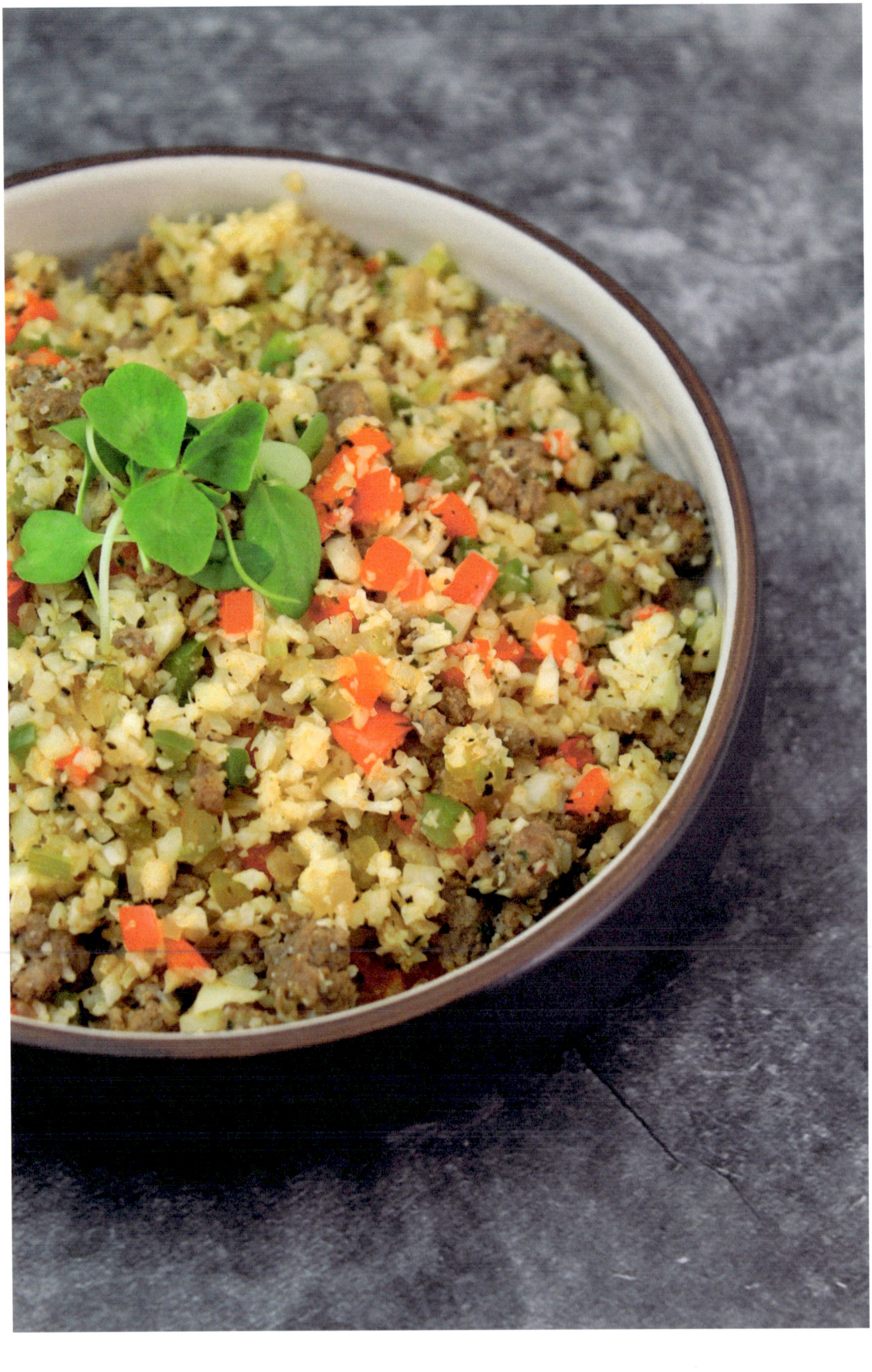

# Dirty Cauliflower Rice

*Serves:* 2  *Prep time:* 35 min  *Total time:* 35 min

---

3 cups cauliflower rice (fresh)
½ cup red pepper diced
½ cup green pepper diced
¼ cup celery diced
¼ cup red onion diced
1 ½ tbsp rough chopped parsley
1 lb ground beef
1 tbsp mushroom umami seasoning
1 tbsp chicken bouillon
1 tsp dried oregano
1 tbsp thyme
¼ tsp paprika
2 bay leaves
1 tbsp minced garlic
1 tsp coarse ground pepper
¼ cayenne

Using a wide pot, on medium heat, cook your ground beef with the umami seasoning, onion, chicken bouillon, oregano, thyme, paprika, bay leaves, garlic, ground pepper and cayenne.

Add the cauliflower rice, red pepper, green pepper and celery to the mix. Stir until the cauliflower is cooked. Turn off the heat and serve immediately.

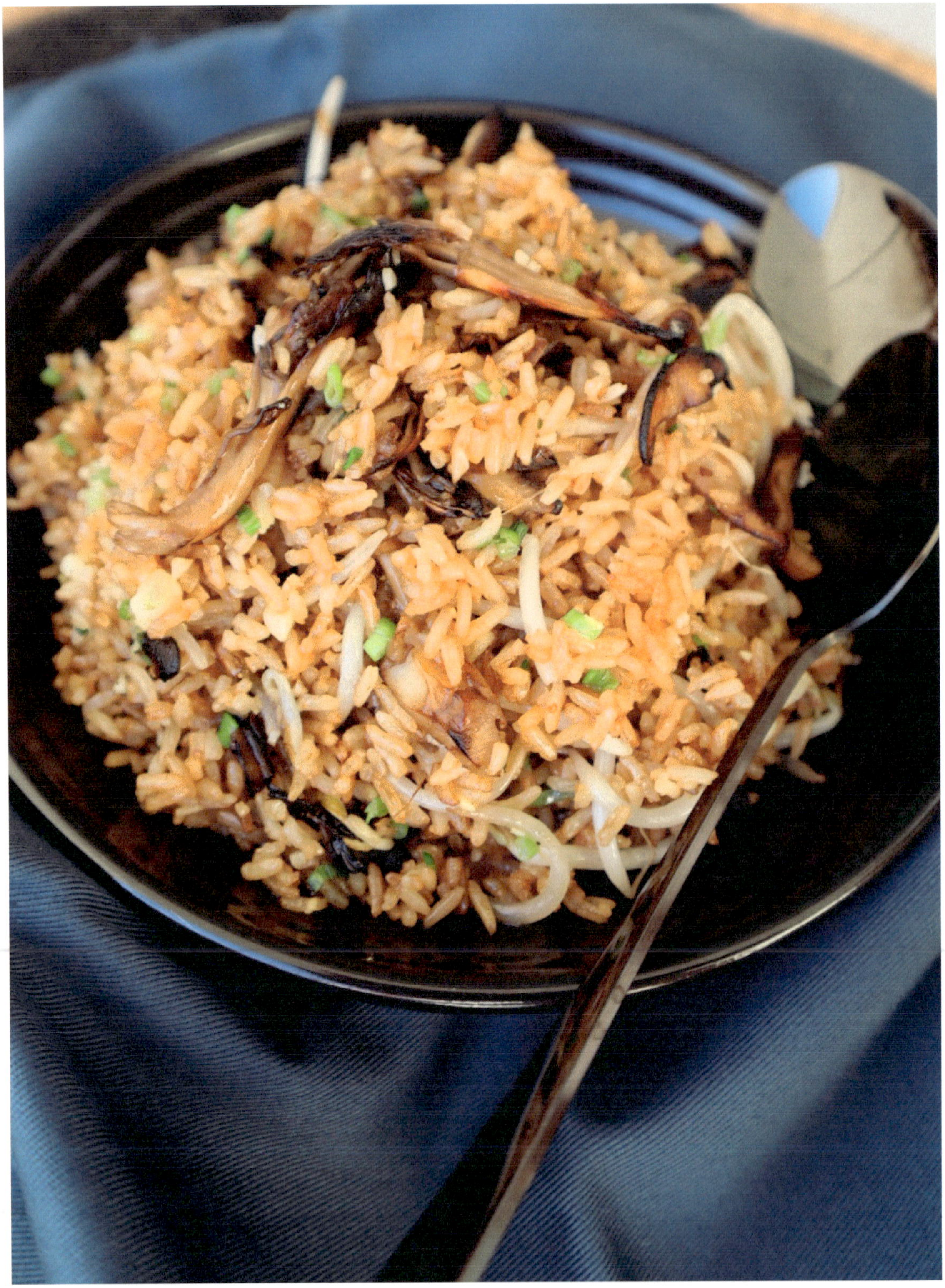

# Mushroom Fried Rice

*Serves:* 2    *Prep time:* 25 min    *Total time:* 25 min

---

1 head maitake mushrooms
1/2 cup shiitake mushrooms
1 tbsp worcestershire sauce
4 tbsp olive oil
1 ½ tsp minced garlic
1 ½ tsp minced ginger
2 cups cold cooked white rice
2 tbsp tamari soy sauce
1 tbsp light sesame oil
1/2 cup thin sliced scallion
1/2 cup bean sprouts

In a large saute pan or wok, add 2 tbsp olive oil and the mushrooms, cook the mushrooms for 12 minutes, giving a constant stir, remove from the heat.

Add the aromatics to the pan with 2 tbsp olive oil on low heat.

Add rice, sesame oil and soy sauce. Saute for 6 minutes, giving vigorous shakes through the saute process.

As the rice is finishing up, add the scallions and bean sprouts.

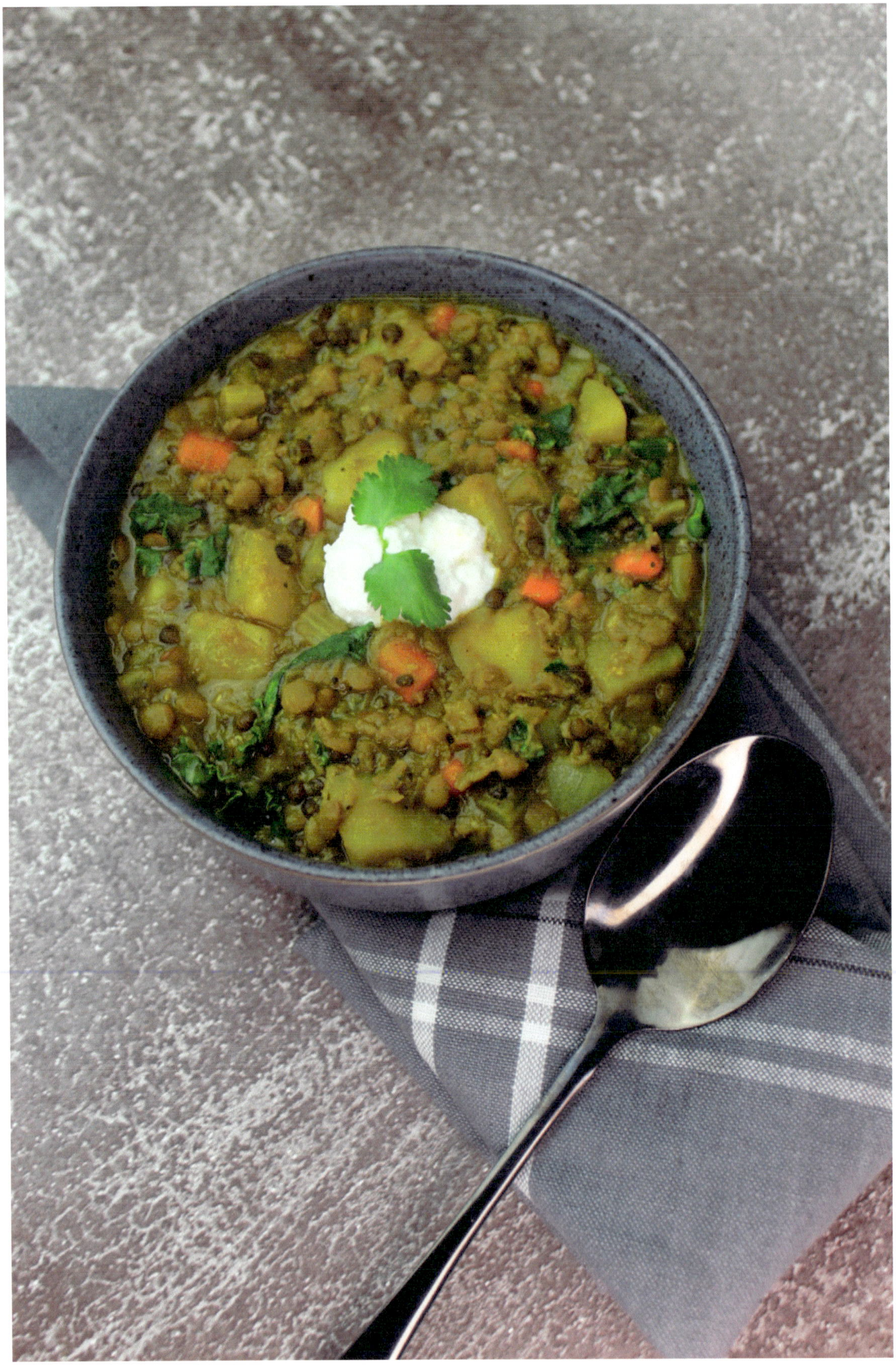

# Curry Lentil Soup

**Serves:** 6    **Prep time:** 12 min    **Total time:** 1 hr

---

2 tbsp olive oil
1 cup lentils
½ cup carrots diced
½ cup onion diced
1 medium potato diced
4 sprigs of thyme
1 tbsp minced garlic
1 slice of ginger
1 tsp turmeric
1 tbsp curry powder
1 tsp cumin
1 tbsp mushroom umami seasoning
3 cups of water
¼ cup coconut milk
1 tsp black pepper
1 ½ tbsp kosher
2 cups of chopped kale (reserve for the very end)

Using a large pot, add the oil, onion, carrots, celery, potato, thyme, curry powder, turmeric, cumin, garlic and ginger. Stir and allow the aromatics to marry for 3-4 minutes.

Add the water, coconut milk, salt, pepper, lentils and umami seasoning. Cook for 30 minutes. The lentils and potato will be tender but yet have a slight bite.

Add the kale and turn off the heat.

Serve the bowl of deliciousness asap with a dollop of vegan whipped cream

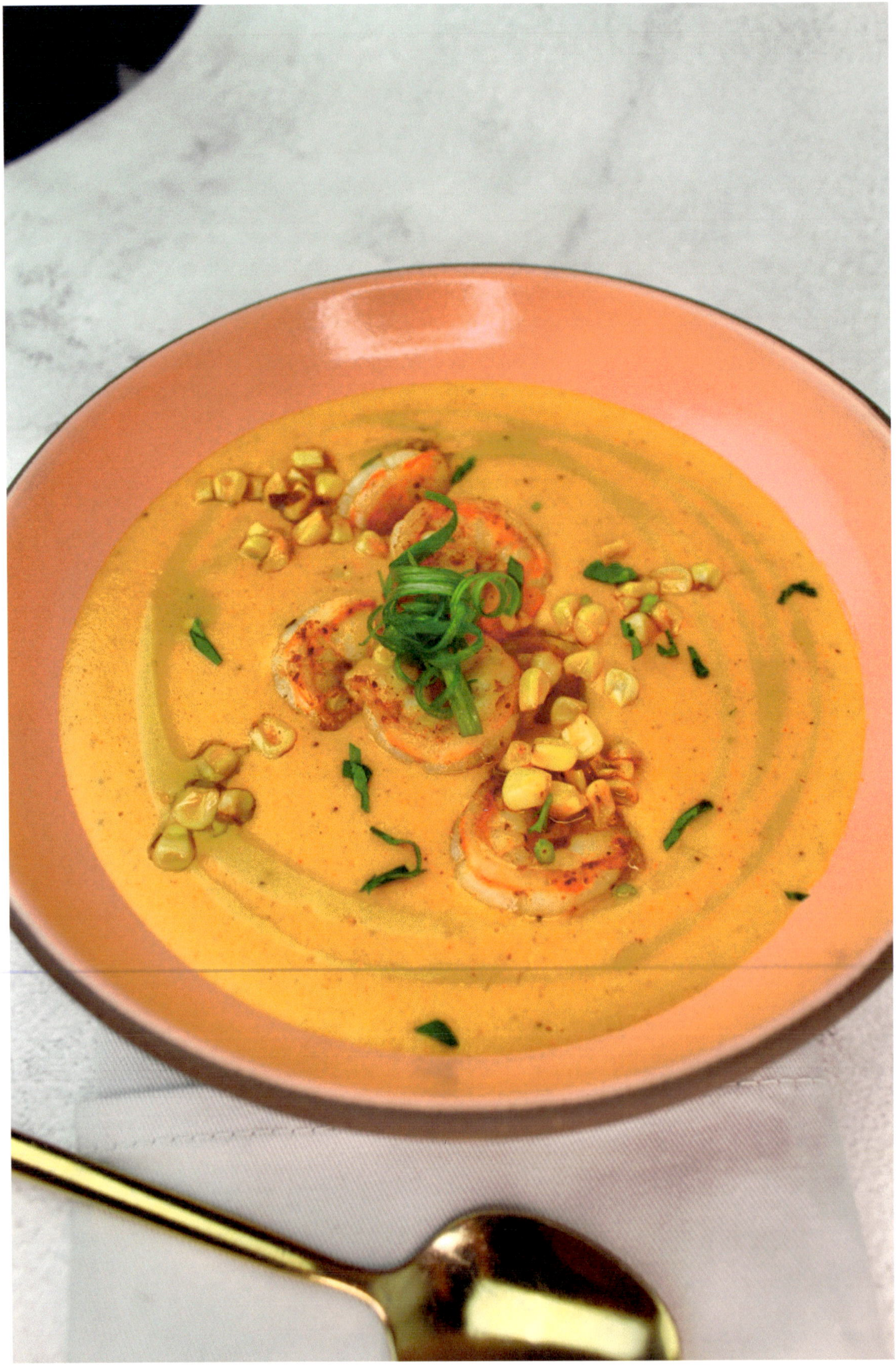

# Shrimp Bisque

**Serves:** 2     **Prep time:** 1 hr     **Total time:** 1 hr

---

2 tbsp olive oil
1 large tomato
2 celery sticks
3 sprigs of thyme
1 carrot
½ onion
6 cloves garlic
1 ear of corn shaved (reserve the kernels for garnish)
1 cup shrimp shells
2 tbsp Old Bay
2 bay leaves
1 cup water
1 ½ cup heavy cream
1 tsp kosher salt
½ lb shrimp
1 tsp cajun seasoning

Shave the kernels off the ear of corn and set aside.

Peel the shrimp, clean and set aside.(reserve the shells)

Using a medium size pot on low to medium heat, add 1 tbsp olive oil, tomato, celery, thyme, carrot, onion, garlic, the remaining ear of corn, shrimp shells and bay leaves, saute for 3 minutes.

Add the water, cream and spices. Cook for 25 minutes on low.

Remove the bay leaves, ear of corn and put all ingredients into a blender. Be careful to start the blender at a low speed with a kitchen towel over the top.This process should only be done with the blender half full to minimize pressure.

Once the bisque is blended, strain the liquid back into the pot using an extremely fine sieve.

Saute the shrimp and corn kernels with the cajun seasoning and olive oil.

Place the soup in a bowl and garnish with the shrimp and corn.

82

# Fortified Fish sauce & Ramen

*Serves:* 2 - 4   ***Prep time:*** *10 min*   ***Total time:*** *1 hr*

---

Carcass of one snapper
6 pcs of scallion
¼ medium onion
1 peeled carrot
6 sprigs of thyme
8 garlic cloves
1 inch knob of ginger
Smashed
6 stems of parsley
1 tbsp miso
1 tbsp gochujang
1 tbsp EVOO
5 cups water
2 tbsp vinegar
1 tbsp soy sauce
3 tbsp kosher salt

Place all ingredients into a large pot and cook on a high to medium heat for 30 minutes, uncovered. This will create a violent boil but that's exactly what you want for this soup.

Remove the majority of the fish carcass and discard. Add half of the liquid to a blender and blend, starting with a low speed and gradually make your way up to a higher speed. Strain using a fine sieve and repeat with the remaining liquid.

Allow the fully strained liquid to simmer for an additional 15 minutes. Place your prepared ramen noodles in a bowl and pour the fish broth over the noodles. Garnish with sesame oil, sliced scallions and cilantro. Enjoy immediately.

84

85

86

87

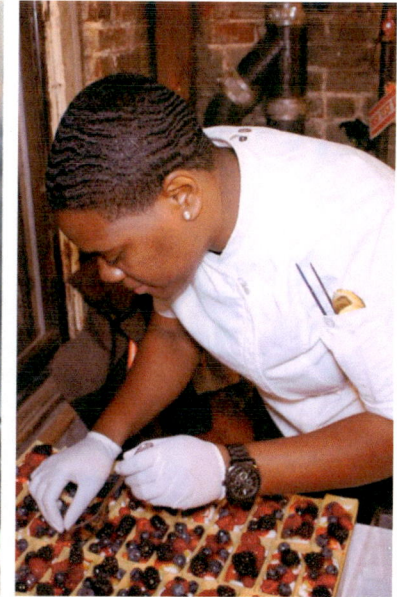

88

89

90

Deconstructed chocolate cake w/ salted caramel candied ginger & bourbon whipped cream

Buttermilk fired chicken bao bun w/ gochujang sweet chili glaze, wasabi soy aioli and fresh herbs

Tuna tartare w/ pear, shallot, tamari,
caviar & truffle wasabi avocado crema

Angel hair pasta w/ Chadon Beni infused tomato sauce & lightly butter kissed smoked crab w/ caviar

Orange, strawberries & cream filled choux au craquelin

Red velvet bread pudding
w/ cream cheese frosting

Soy glazed A5 Wagyu w/mango salsa & chipotle aioli

in a fused nouri, rice paper taco

Spicy salmon tartare w/ salmon roe

Black sesame cone w/ kimchi salmon tartare & wasabi avocado mousse

Seared scallop w/chorizo avocado mousse, serrano peppers, wasabi roe, mango salsa & citrus salt

Baby gem caesar salad w/ spiced corn bread crumble miso caesar dressing & shaved parm

Fondant potato w/ shrimp paste, sriracha aioli, red pepper coulis, scallions, serrano pepper & sesame

# Grab a Plate

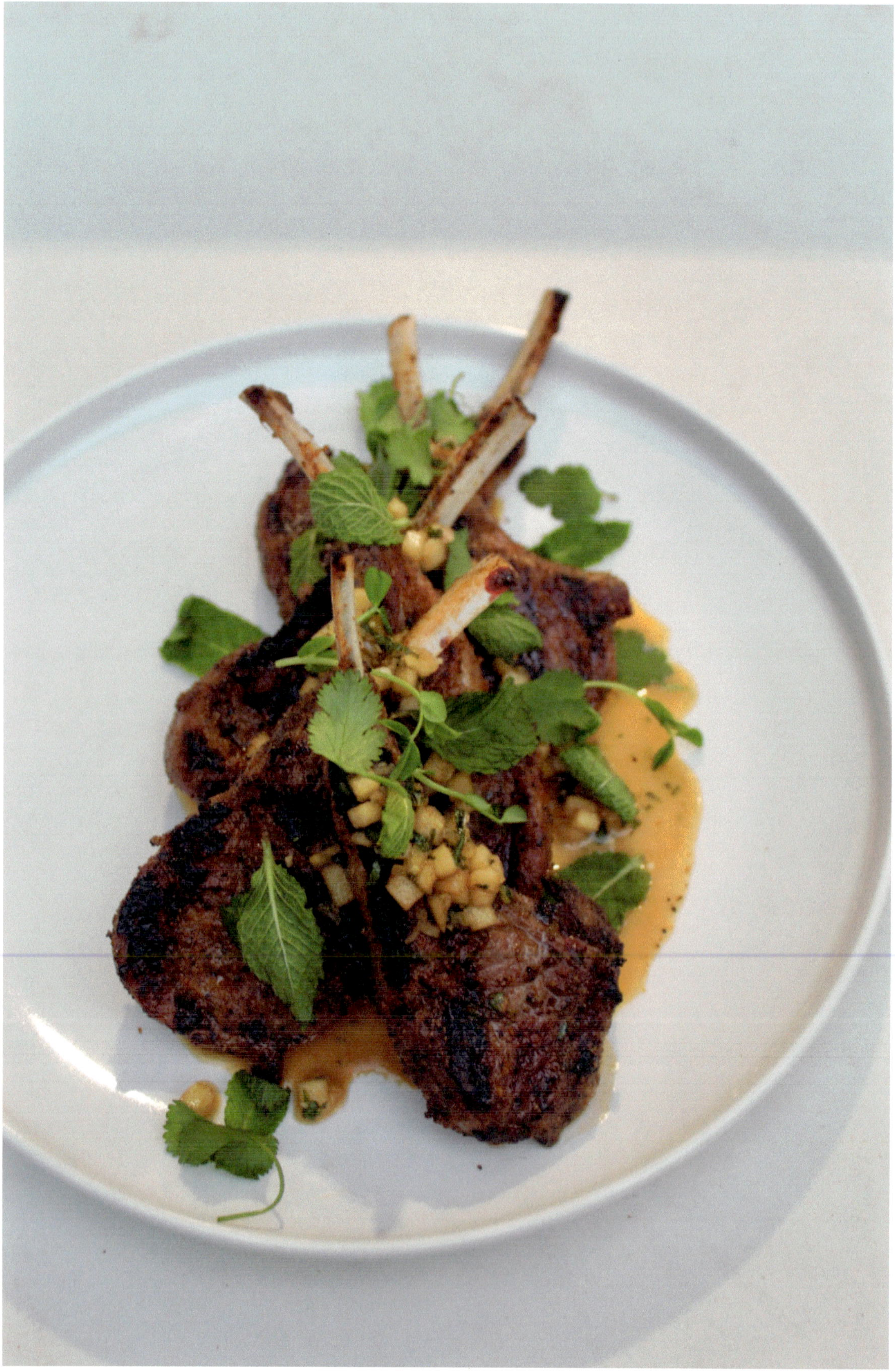

# Grilled lamb w/Pear & shallot gastrique

**Serves:** 2    **Prep time:** 1 hr    **Total time:** 2.5 hr

---

Marinade
6 lamb chops
1 tbsp umami seasoning
⅛ tsp clove
¼ tsp paprika
½ tsp cumin
1 tsp granulated garlic
½ tsp ground black pepper
½ tsp sugar
2 tbsp EVOO

Gastrique
½ diced small
½ shallot finely diced
1 tsp cilantro finely chopped
5 mint leaves finely julienned
1 tsp finely minced ginger
2 tsp sesame oil
2 tsp honey
3 tsp tamari soy sauce
2 tsp water
Juice of ½ lime
4 tbsp butter

In a large mixing bowl marinade the lamb with the spices and olive oil for 2 hrs or more.

For the gastrique, add the sesame oil, honey, soy, water and lime juice to a small saucepan and cook on a low heat for 5- 7 minutes.

Add the cold butter 1 tbsp at a time, slowly stirring. Remove from the heat. Allow to cool, then add the herbs, pear and shallots.

Grill the lamb for 3 minutes on each side at 375 degrees. Your level of preferred doneness takes precedence in this recipe.

Once the lamb is finished, plate the lamb and pour the gastrique over the dish.

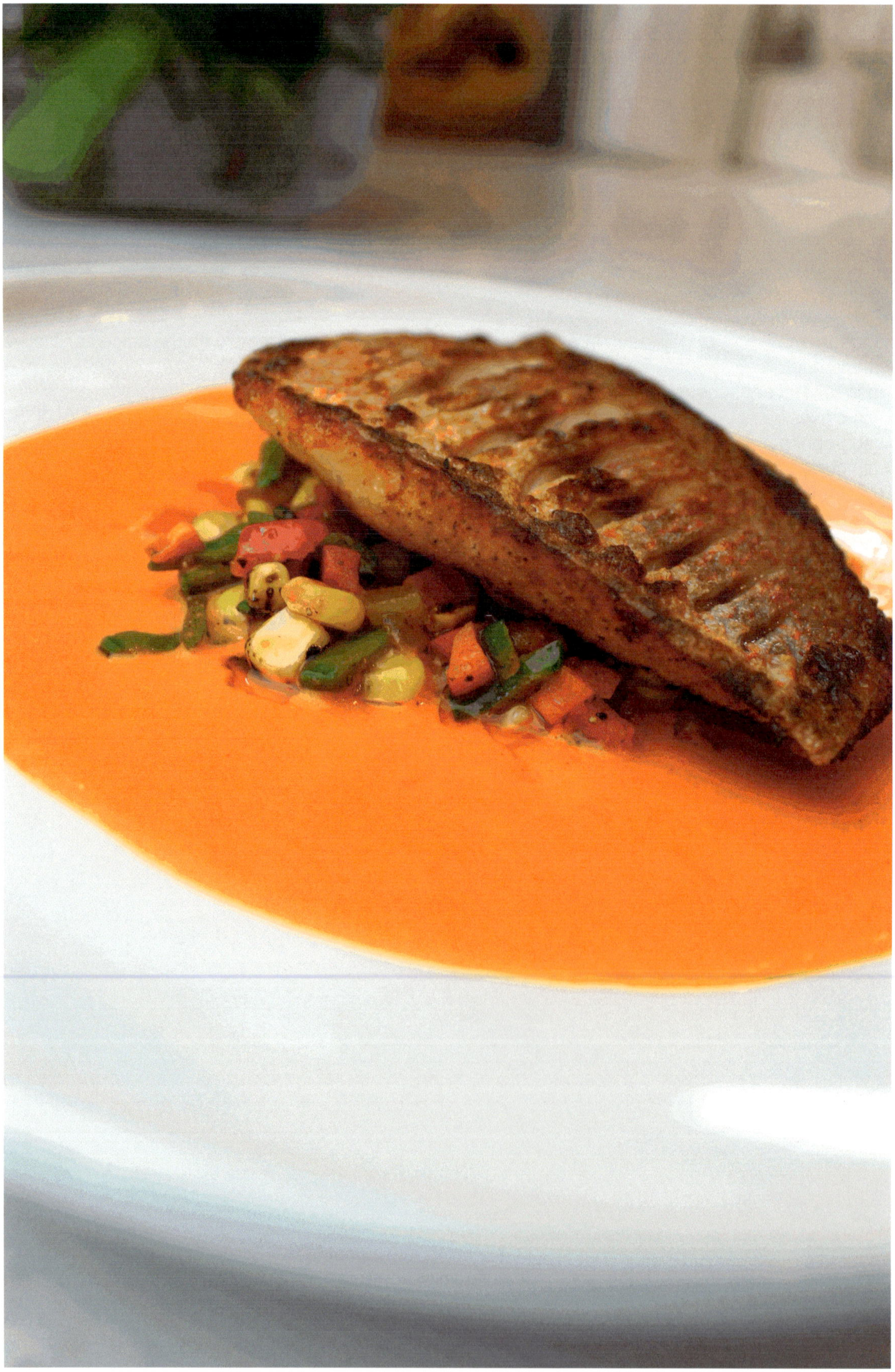

# Pan Seared Snapper w/ Succotash

**Serves:** 2    **Prep time:** 1 hr    **Total time:** 12 hrs

---

**Soak**
2 lb whole red snapper
1 lime
1 tbsp salt
2 cups water

**Fish Seasoning**
1 tsp granulated garlic
½ tsp salt
1 tsp berber
1 tsp sugar

**Succotash**
¼ cup Fresh Corn
¼ cup snow peas small cuts
¼ cup red pepper diced small
¼ cup red onion diced small
¼ cup carrot diced small
3 tbsp compound butter

**Red Pepper Curry Cream sauce**
½ red pepper
1 cup water
1 tsp curry powder
4 garlic cloves
½ tsp Kosher salt
½ cup heavy cream
2 tbsp butter

**Compound butter**
4 tbsp room temp butter
2 scallions chopped
½ tbsp gochujang
1 tsp herb de provence
1 tsp Kosher salt

Make slits in the flesh of the fish. Place in a bowl with the salt, water and lime juice for 30 minutes.

Rinse the fish, pat dry and season with the berbere, paprika, cumin & garlic. Let the fish air dry in the fridge overnight.

Mix all ingredients for the compound butter and place in the fridge until ready for use.

Preparation of the red pepper curry cream sauce is simple. In a small saucepan, cook the garlic and red pepper in water for 20 minutes, add the garlic, red pepper and remaining water to a blender and blend until smooth. Add the ingredients back to the saucepan add the cream, butter and salt. Stir and simmer for 5 minutes

Using a saute pan, on medium heat add a tbsp of olive oil and add a piece of parchment paper, then add one more tbsp of olive oil before placing the fish skin side down. Using care, as you put the fish down, use a spatula and press down gently for 25 seconds, the flesh of the fish should relax.

Cook for 4 minutes and flip onto the flesh side. Cook for an additional 3 minutes.

For the vegetable succotash, add 2 tbsp of the compound butter into a medium saute pan and cook the vegetable for 3 minutes. While we are aiming for tenderness, we still want a bite that gives texture.

Plate by placing the sauce down, followed by the succotash and topping with the fish.

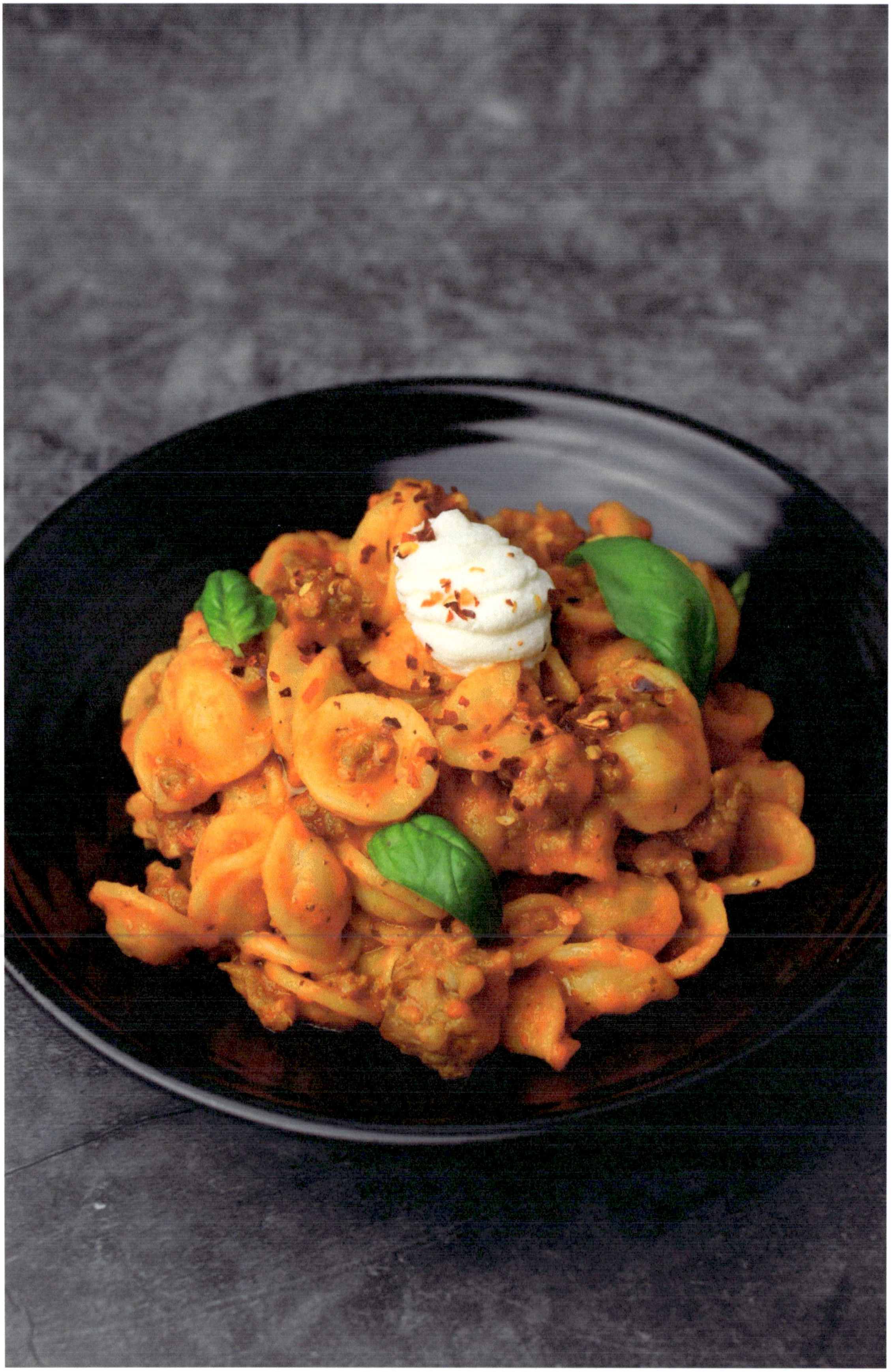

# Red Pepper Pasta

*Serves:* 4  *Prep time:* 55 min  *Total time:* 1 hr

---

1 lb hot italian sausage
½ large onion diced
1 red pepper
15 oz can of tomato
5 cloves of garlic
1 ¼ cup water
½ tsp smoked paprika
1 tsp fennel seed
¼ tsp cumin
1 tsp red wine vinegar
1 tsp herb de provence
1 tsp granulated garlic
3 tbsp butter (add when sauce is just about finished)
3 cups orecchiette pasta
Fresh basil

Using a large pot, cook the sausage for 5 minutes and remove from the pan.

Add the remaining ingredients for the sauce and cook for 20 minutes. It's fine if you didn't remove all of the sausage bits out of the pan, this adds flavor.

Once the sauce is cooked, carefully add to a blender. Keep a towel on the top of the lid. Friendly reminder, don't add hot liquids past the halfway mark in the blender.

Add the sauce and the sausage back to the pot and simmer for an additional 15 minutes.

While the sauce is finishing, bring a pot of water to a rolling boil and salt heavily.

Add the orecchiette pasta and cook for 5 minutes. Drain and reserve ½ cup water.

Using a saute pan, add the sauce and pasta. Give a light toss and allow to simmer for 5 minutes.

Garnish with basil and enjoy.

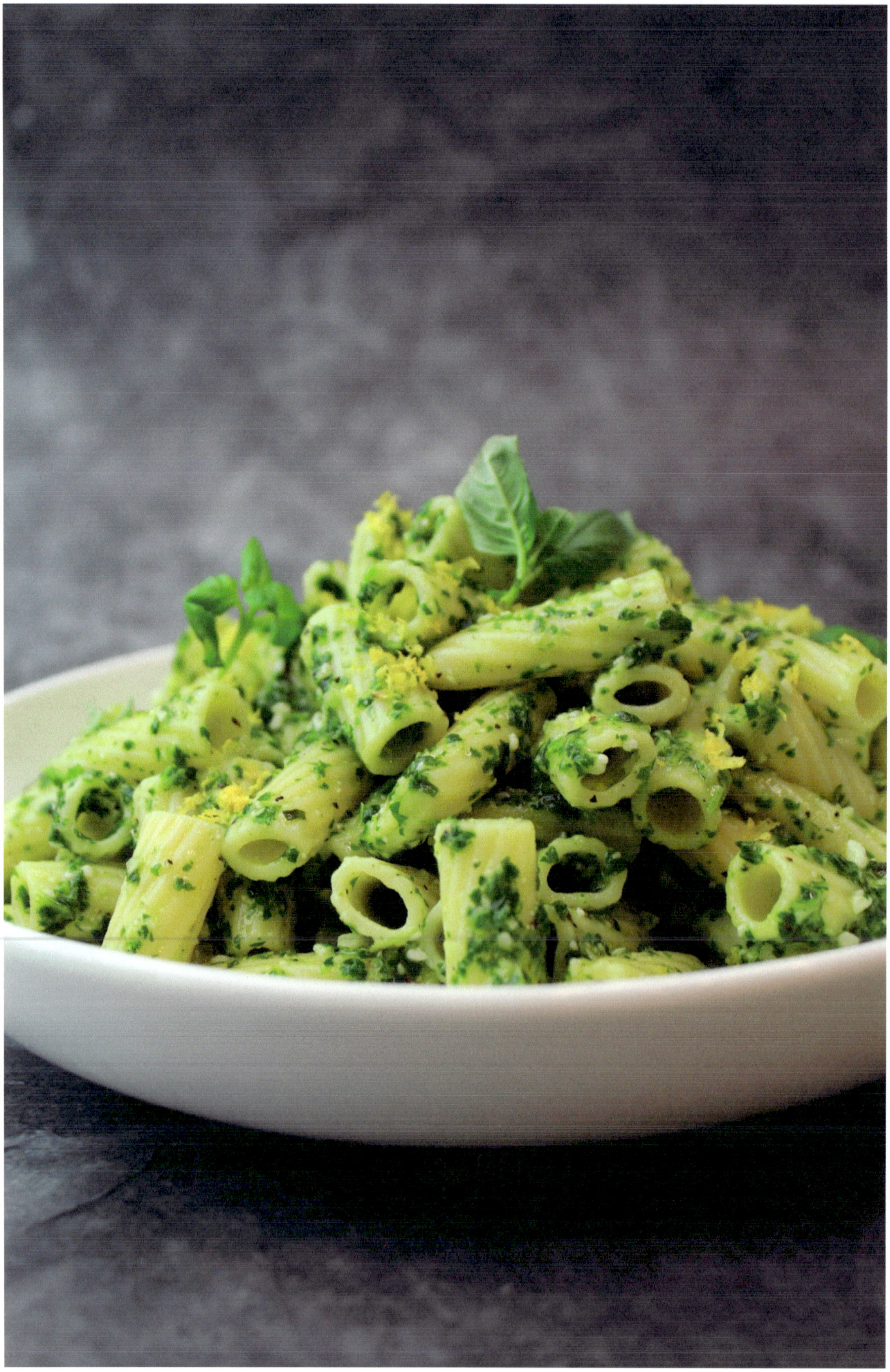

# Arugula Pesto Pasta

*Serves:* 2  *Prep time:* 20 min  *Total time:* 25 min

**Pesto**
5 oz pack of arugula
1 cup of basil leaves
1 bulb of garlic peeled
2 oz pecorino cheese or vegan parmesan
1 tbsp coarse ground pepper
1 tbsp salt
6 oz oil
Juice of 1 lemon

Add all of the ingredients for the pesto into a food processor except the oil.

Heat a pot of water and bring to a rolling boil. Heavily salt your water and cook your pasta of choice for 9 minutes, drain and toss with the pesto.

Shave lemon zest to add some extra brightness.

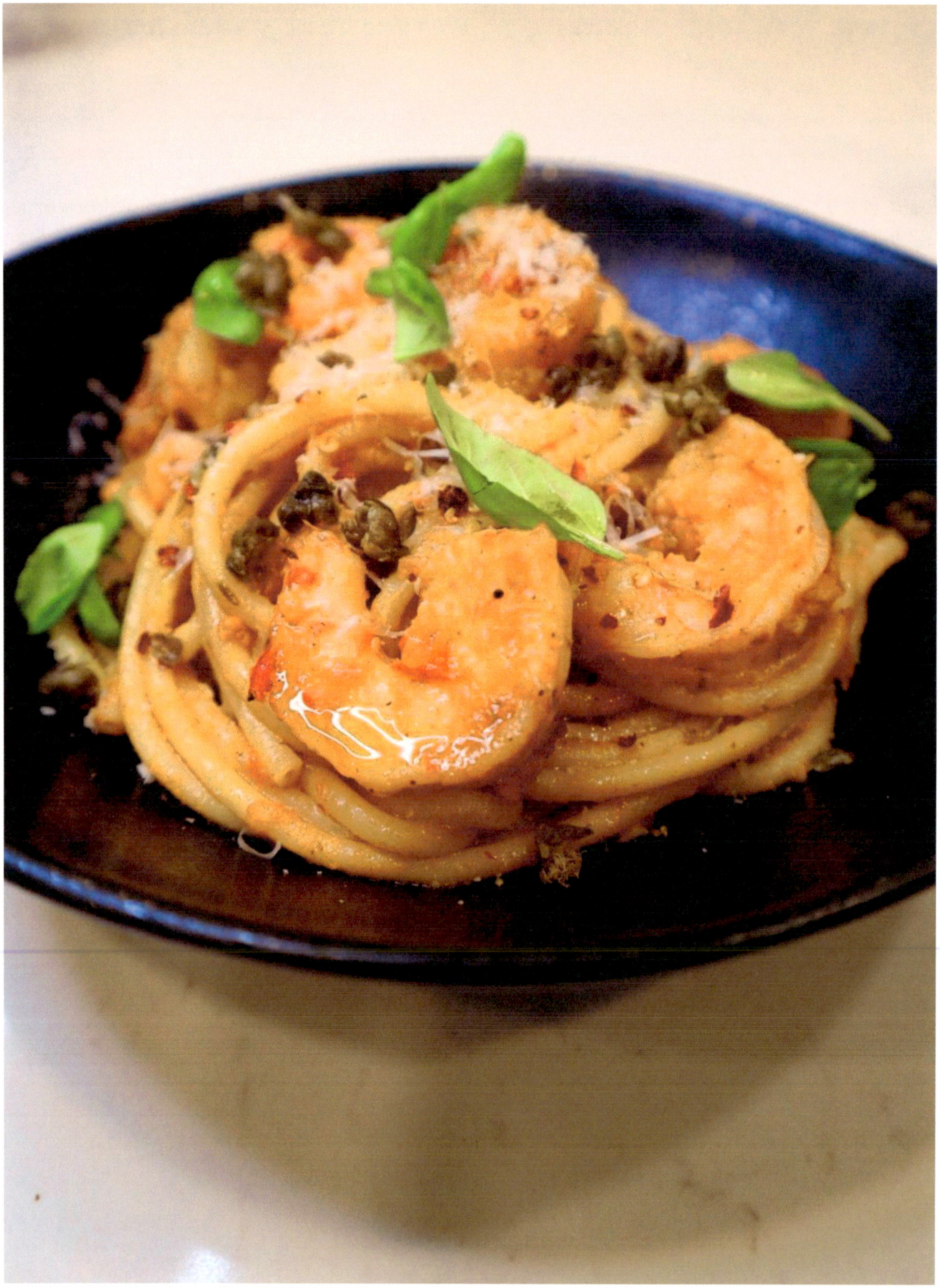

# Shrimp Fra Diavolo

*Serves:* 4     *Prep time:* 45 min     *Total time:* 1.5 hr

---

**Sauce**
4 roma or vine tomatoes
1 Bulb of garlic peeled
1 Medium sized onion
1 fresno pepper
1 stick of butter
1 tsp Cumin
2 tbsp Red pepper flakes
4 tbsp Kosher salt
2 tbsp Sugar
1 tbsp Herb de provence
1 tbsp Fennel seed
Zest of one lemon
1 tbsp of fresh oregano
6 leaves of basil, thinly sliced aka chiffonade
1/2 cup of white wine

**Shrimp**
24 jumbo shrimp (peeled and deveined)
1 tsp granulated garlic
1 tsp black pepper
1 tsp paprika
1 tsp kosher salt

Smash the garlic gloves, cut the tomatoes in half and quarter the onions, season liberally with salt pepper and olive oil.

Roast in the oven at 400 degrees for 45 min.

Once the veggies are roasted, place in a food processor and pulse until a few chunks remain.

Add the sauce to the pot and place on low simmer for 20 minutes.

From there add your spices, herbs and white wine to enhance the flavors.

Bring a large pot of water to a boil and salt heavily.

Allow your pasta to cook until al dente (every brand has different instructions, follow accordingly).

Strain and reserve ½ cup of the pasta water.

Mix the dry ingredients together and coat the shrimp adding a few drizzles of olive oil (set in the fridge for 15 min and lightly coat with all purpose flour.

Using a saute pan, add olive oil and cook the shrimp on each side for 2 - 3 mins, remove from the pan, add your prepared sauce and a good amount of pasta water.

Add the pasta and the shrimp and gently toss to finish cooking. Place on a plate add capers, freshly shaved parmesan and fresh basil.

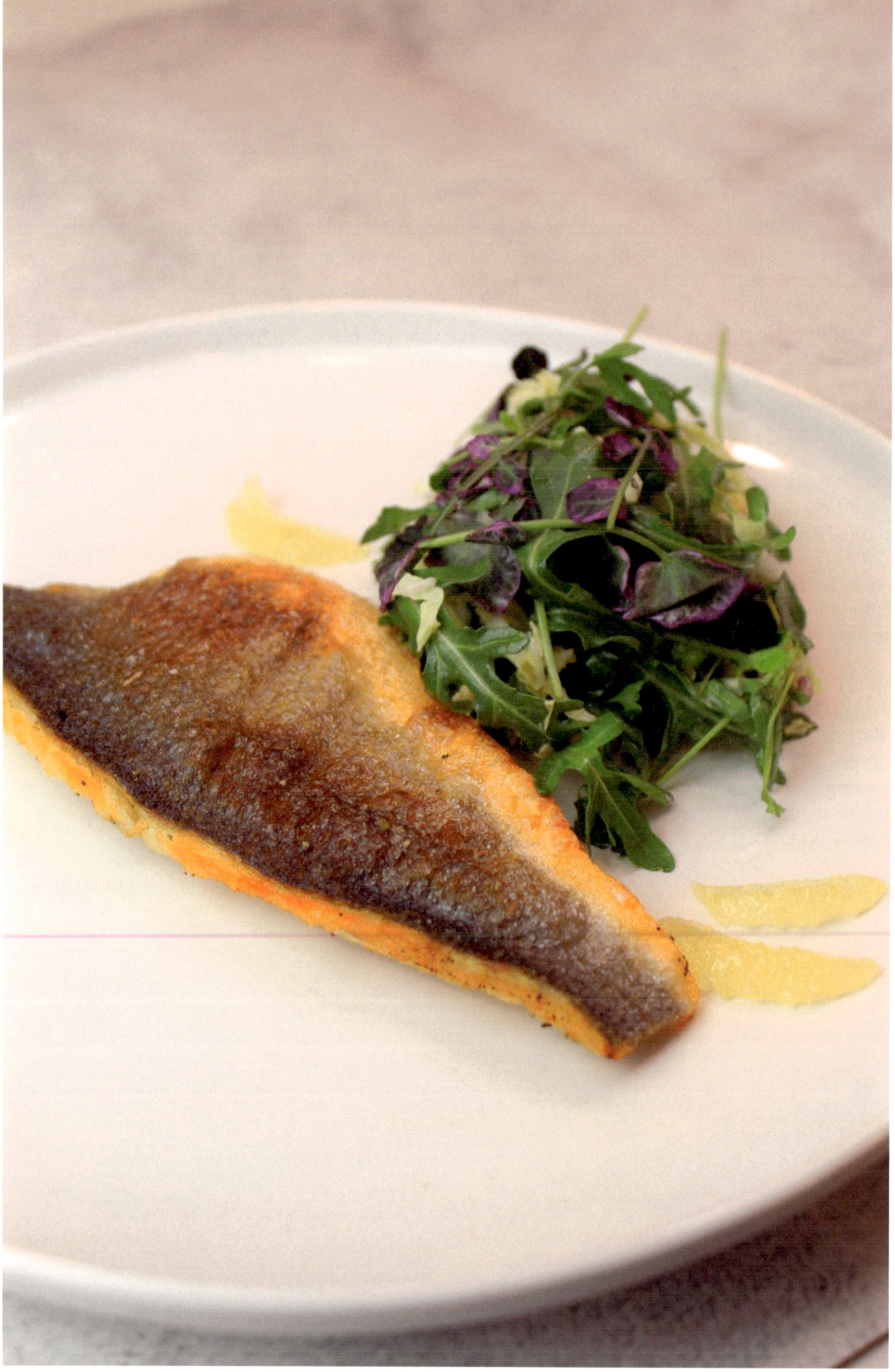

# Branzino w/ Watercress salad

***Serves:*** *2*  ***Prep time:*** *30 min*  ***Total time:*** *40 min*

---

**Branzino**
½ tsp kosher salt
½ tsp coarse ground pepper
½ tsp granulated garlic
2 large branzino fillets

**Salad**
1 cup watercress
1 cup arugula
1 ½ cup napa cabbage (thinly sliced)
Lemon (reserve for the end)
1 tsp sugar

**Dressing**
¼ shallot finely minced
1 ½ tbsp olive oil
1 tsp thyme leaves
1 tbsp honey
1 tbsp lemon juice

Pat dry the branzino and season with salt, pepper and granulated garlic.

Supreme the lemon using a paring knife to cut off the top and bottom, stand the lemon up on the exposed flesh, remove the skin by taking your knife from the top to the bottom following the curve around the lemon until all flesh is exposed.

From there you will cut out the segments by using the knife to cut along the interior of the membrane, creating a V.

For the salad, add all ingredients to the bowl except the lemon and sugar. In a separate bowl, add the sugar to the lemon and allow the sugars to penetrate the lemon to reduce acid. You will add the lemon to the salad as you are building the dish.

To make the dressing, add the thyme, shallot, lemon juice, salt and honey. Using your whisk, slowly add the oil to create a light dressing.

Using a saute pan on medium heat, add 1 tbsp of olive oil and allow the oil to get hot. Place your fish skin side down, use a fish spatula to press the fish down to prevent curling. Cook for 2-3 minutes on each side.

Remove from the heat, dress your salad and serve immediately.

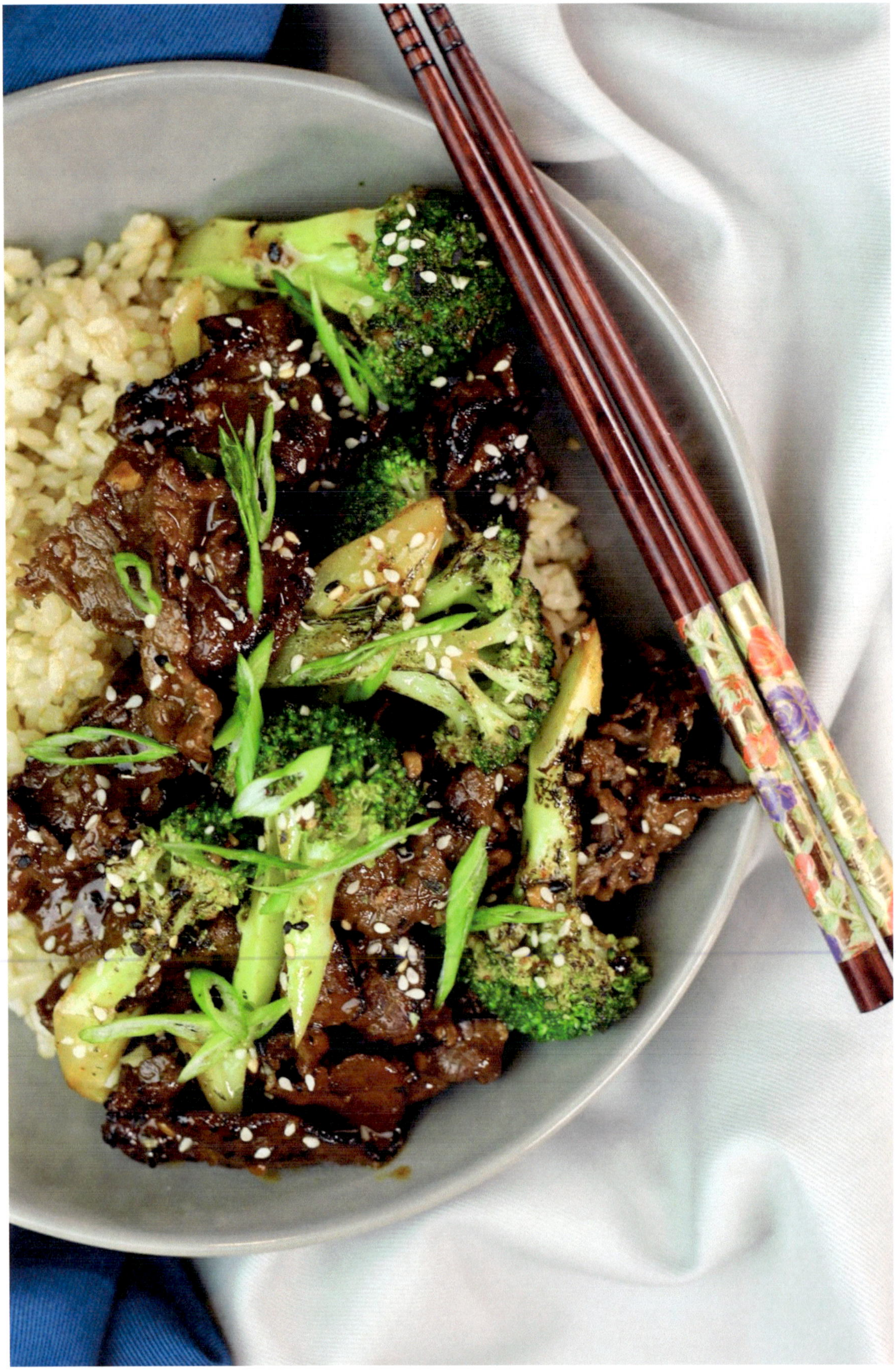

# Beef & Broccoli w/ Brown Rice

**Serves:** 2    **Prep time:** 30 min    **Total time:** 1 hr

---

**Brown rice**
1 ½ cups of brown rice
1 tbsp olive oil
1 tsp kosher salt
3 cups of water

**Beef**
8oz beef round sliced thinly
1/2 tbsp garlic powder
1/2 tbsp coarse ground pepper
1/2 tbsp sesame oil
1/2 tbsp low sodium soy sauce

**Sauce**
1/2 tsp olive oil
1 tbsp minced garlic
1 tbsp minced ginger
2 tbsp sugar
1/8 tsp ground ginger
1/2 cup of water
1/2 cup tamari soy sauce
1 tbsp cornstarch

½ head of broccoli
Thinly sliced scallions for garnish

Rinse the rice thoroughly and add 3 cups of water to a pot, cover and cook on low for 40 mins. The rice will be tender and have a slight bite to it.

Cut the broccoli into florets and boil for 3 minutes.

Flash in cold water to stop the cooking process, drain and set to the side.

Combine the beef, garlic, powder, pepper, sesame oil and soy sauce in a bowl and marinate for 15 minutes.

Using a saute pan or wok, add 2 tbsp of olive oil and cook the beef for 4 minutes on high heat. Remove from the pan and saute the broccoli in the same pan for 2 minutes, as it absorbs that flavor and set aside.

To build the sauce, add the olive oil to the hot wok, add the garlic and ginger, allow this to perfume for 1 minute on a low heat. Then add the soy sauce, ground ginger and sugar, allow this to marry for 4 minutes on a low to medium heat

In a small bowl, mix the cornstarch and water to make a slurry, slowly add the mixture to the sauce with heat on medium and stir until fully combined. This will quickly thicken your sauce. Cook for 3 minutes.

Add your beef and broccoli to the sauce to fully coat and place on top of your rice. Garnish with thinly sliced scallions and enjoy.

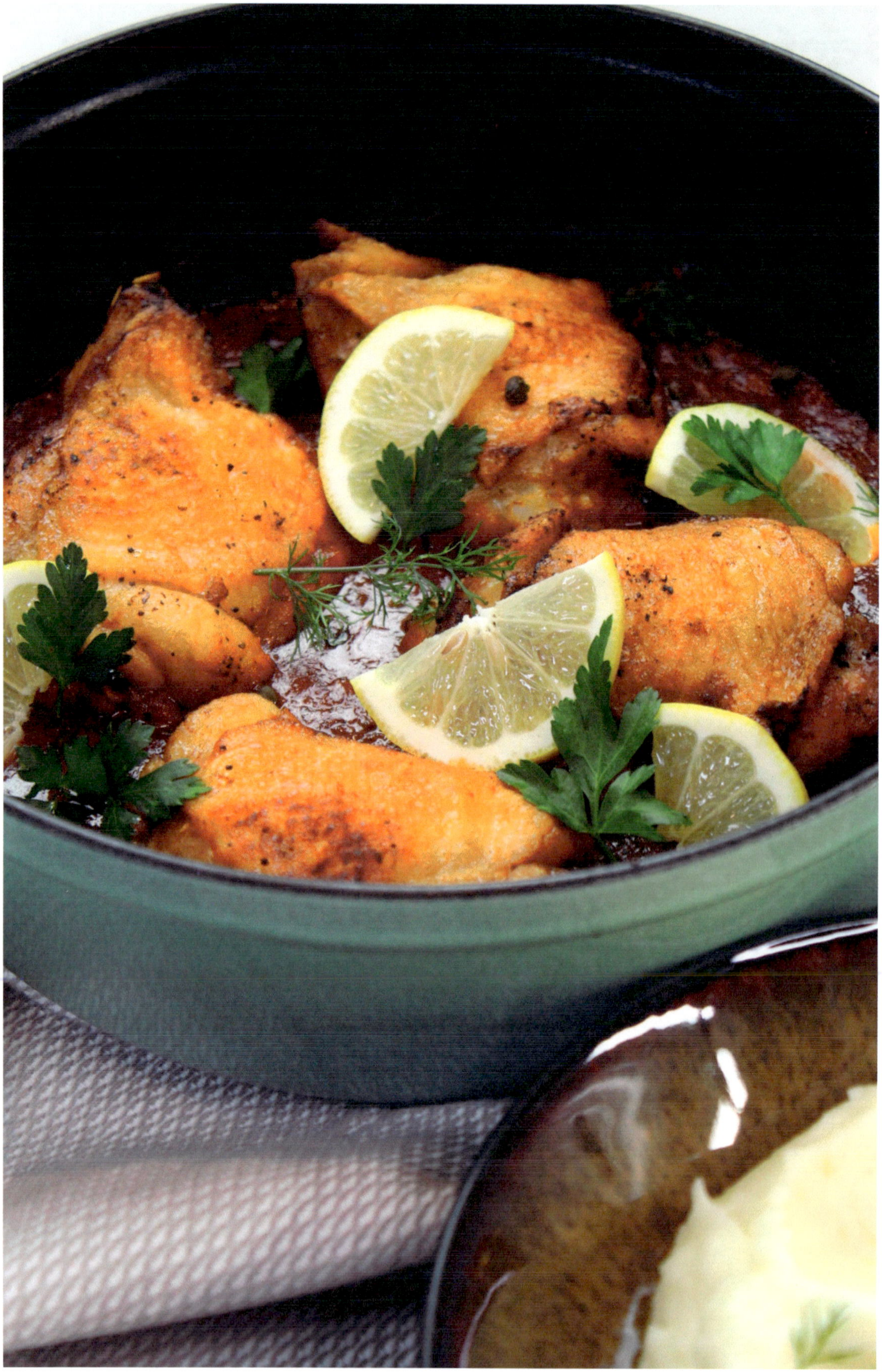

# Roasted Chicken Thighs

*Serves:* 2     *Prep time:* 25 min     *Total time:* 1.5 hr

**Soak**
1 lemon
1 tbsp kosher salt
2 cups water
4 chicken thighs

**Seasoning**
½ tbsp kosher salt
½ tbsp coarse black pepper
½ tbsp granulated garlic
1 tsp salt (for the skin only)

**Sauce**
⅓ cup sundried tomato julienned
½ tsp cumin
⅛ tsp cayenne pepper
1 tsp kosher salt
1 tsp herb de provence
1 tsp granulated garlic
1 tsp smoked paprika
2 tbsp sugar
2 tbsp minced garlic
5 tbsp tomato paste
1 tbsp red wine vinegar
½ tbsp hot sauce
1 cup water
1 shallot thinly sliced
2 tbsp capers

Soak the chicken for 30 minutes in the lemon, salt and water.

Pat the chicken dry and make a few slits in the flesh side of the chicken and season with the salt, granulated garlic and black pepper.

Flip the chicken skin side up and season with salt only.

Using medium to high heat for the dutch oven pot, add 1 ½ tbsp olive oil.

Preheat your oven to 425 degrees.

Sear the chicken skin side down for 4 minutes, turn and cook on the opposite side for 4 minutes and remove from the pan.

Add the remaining ingredients into the pot and simmer for 10 minutes.

Place the chicken on top of the sauce and cook for 30 minutes in the oven uncovered.

Allow to cool slightly and indulge.

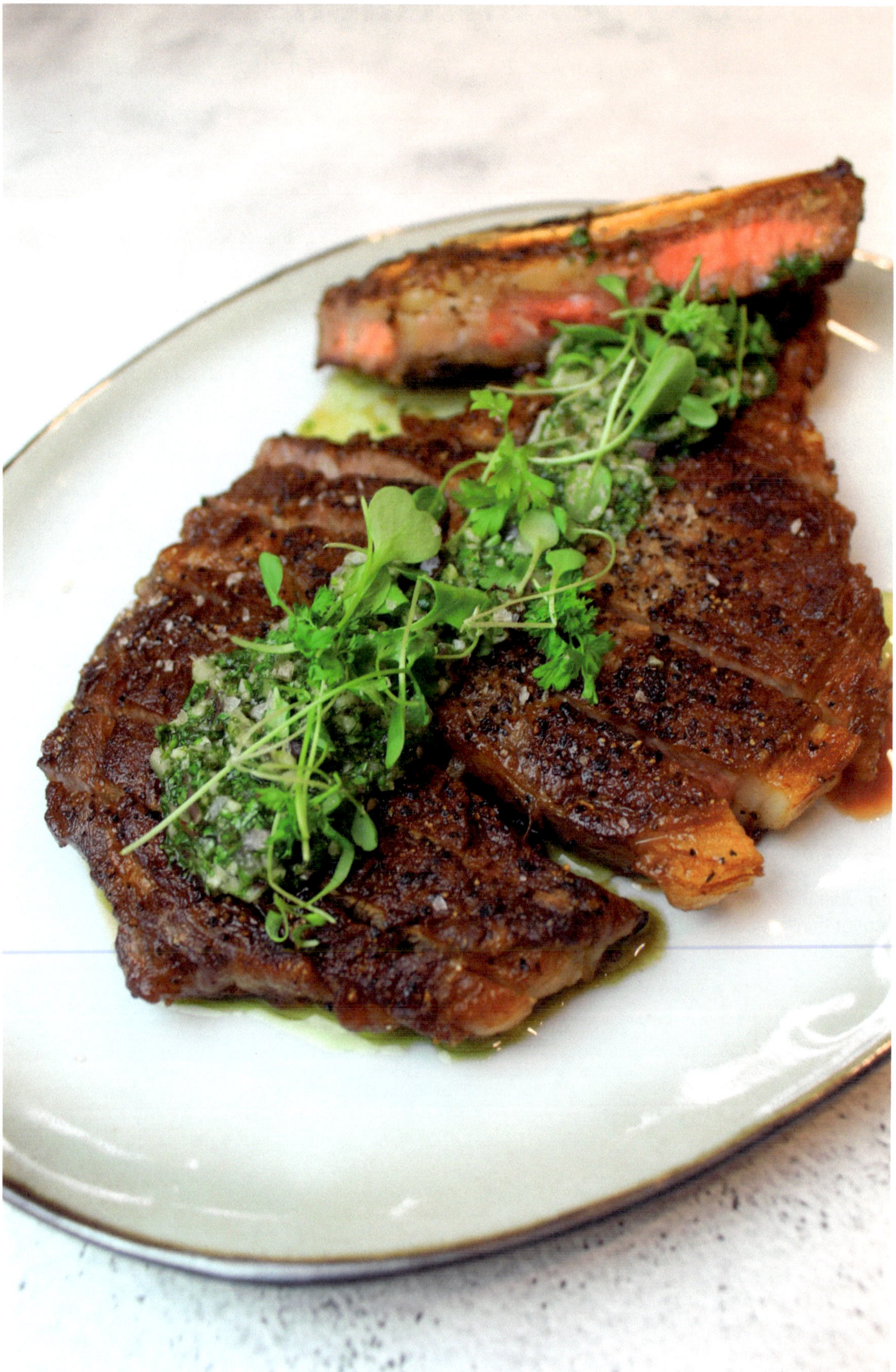

# Rib Eye w/ Chimichurri Sauce

**Serves:** 1     **Prep time:** 25 min     **Total time:** 35 min

---

**Chimichurri**
1/2 cup finely chopped parsley
1/2 cup finely chopped cilantro
1 tbsp finely cut fresno pepper (no seeds) 1/2 of a large red onion finely minced
1 tbsp of honey
4 cloves of garlic finely minced
1/2 cup olive oil
1/2 cup red wine vinegar
kosher salt to taste

**Rib Eye**
7oz rib eye (thick cut)
1 tsp kosher salt
1 tsp black pepper
1 tbsp olive oil
2 tbsp butter
2 sprigs thyme
2 garlic cloves

Combine all the ingredients for the chimichurri in a bowl and store in a leak proof container.

Be sure to pat the steak dry and season with the salt and pepper on both sides.

Heat a cast iron skillet on a medium to high heat, add the oil.

Sear the steak on both sides for 2 minutes.on each side.

Add the butter, sprigs of thyme, smashed garlic gloves and begin basting the steak with the butter. 1 minute on each side to form a dark crust.

Remove from the heat and let the juices settle, slice the steak, add the chimichurri and enjoy.

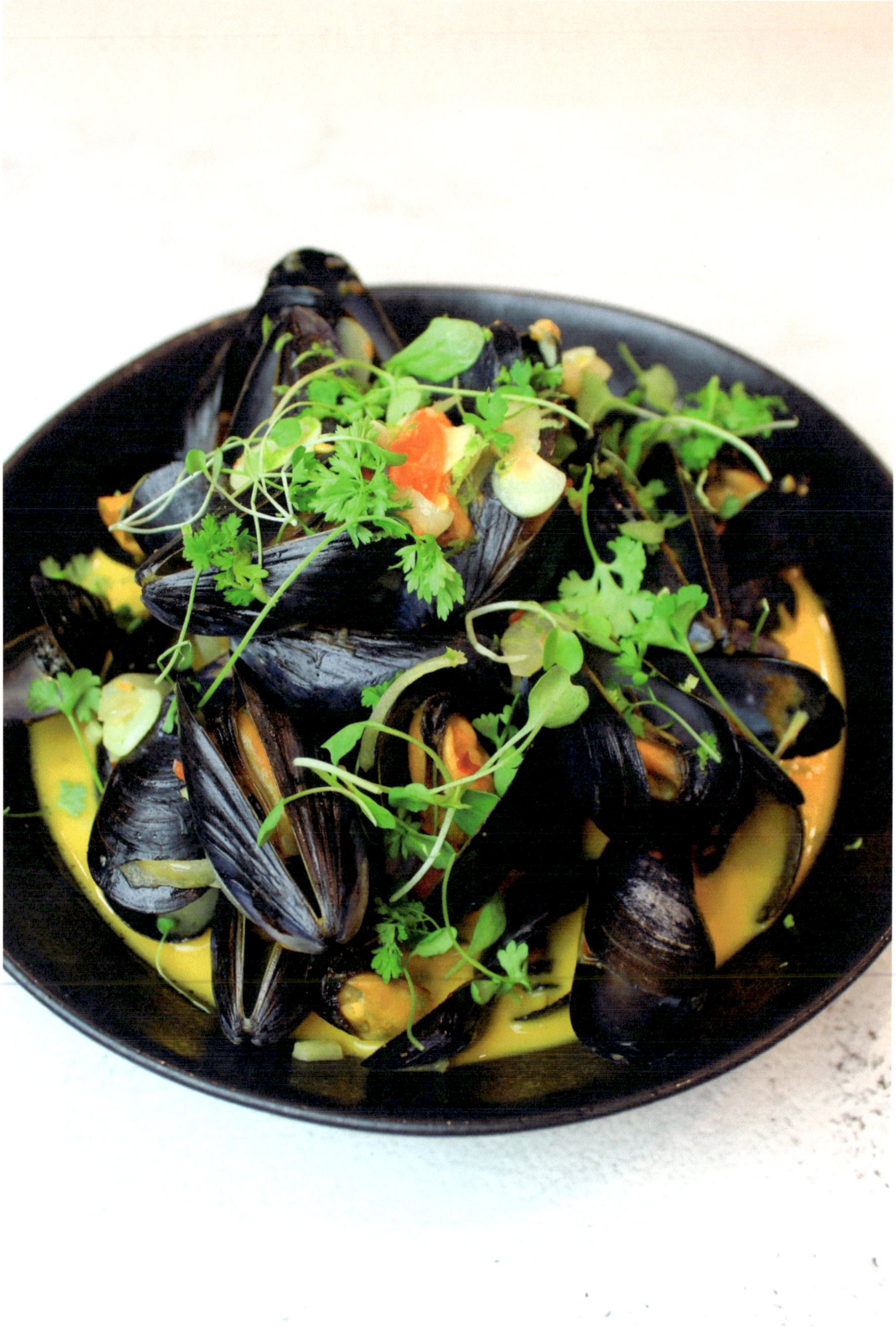

# Harissa Curry Ginger Mussels

*Serves:* 2   *Prep time:* 15 min   *Total time:* 25 min

---

2 lbs mussels (cleaned and debearded)
1 ½ cup white wine
½ cup cream
1 ½ tsp salt
1 tbsp minced ginger
5 cloves of garlic sliced
2 tbsp harissa
1 tsp curry
½ onion thinly sliced
3 tbsp butter
½ cup cherry tomatoes sliced in half
Zest of ½ lime to garnish
Parsley to garnish

Using a large pot on medium heat, add the butter and aromatics; curry, ginger, garlic, onions, saute for 3 minutes and add the tomatoes.

Add the wine, heavy cream and harissa to the pot and simmer for 3 minutes.

Put the mussels in the pot and cover for 8 minutes.

You'll know the mussels are finished when all the shells are open completely.

Discard any mussels that haven't opened completely.

Garnish with parsley and lime zest. Toast a baguette and enjoy that beautiful sauce.

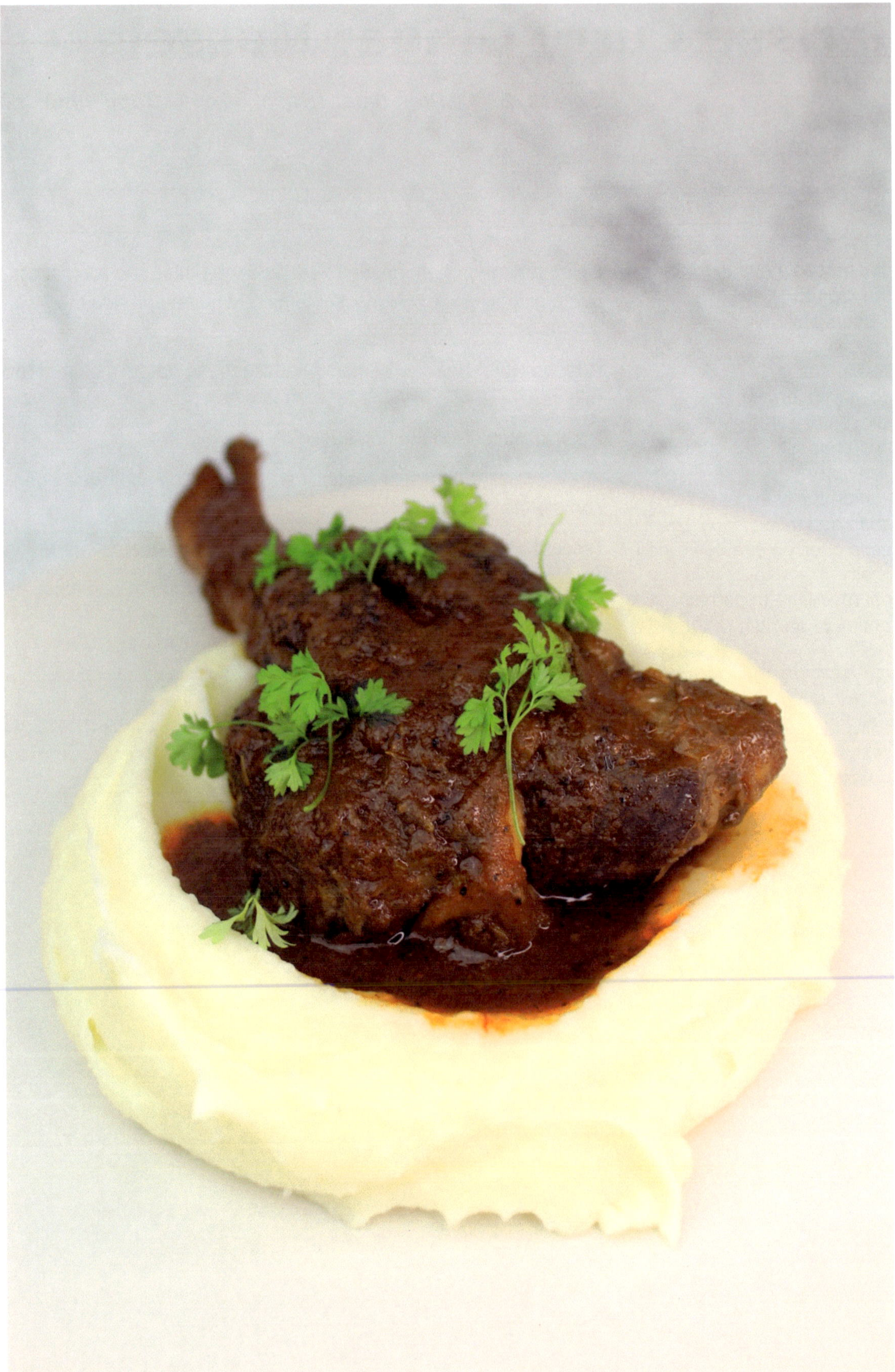

# Braised Lamb Shank

*Serves:* 4    *Prep time:* 24 hrs    *Total time:* 27 hrs

**Seasoning**
4 pc lamb shank
1 ½ tbsp granulated garlic
1 ½ tbsp onion powder
1 ½ tbsp cumin
2 tbsp kosher salt
1 tsp paprika
1/1 tsp cinnamon
2 tbsp olive oil

**Braising liquid**
1 tsp fennel seed
1 ½ onion sliced
3 bay leaves
2 celery sticks bruised (leave whole for removal)
1 cup red wine
2 ⅔ cup water
1 ½ cup tomato sauce
1 ½ tsp curry powder
1 tbsp brown sugar
2 tbsp herb de provence
1 tbsp red wine vinegar
1 tbsp kosher salt
2 tbsp green seasoning
**(See page 46)**
**Mash**
4 cloves garlic
4 pounds potato
½ cup butter
1 cup of cream
Salt to taste

Be sure to remove any excess silver skin for the lamb shanks prior to adding the seasoning and oil. Marinate overnight in a tightly covered bowl.

Using a large pot, add 2 tbsp of olive oil, sear the lamb shank on all sides and remove from the pot.

Add the onion, fennel seed, bay leaves, celery and curry powder. Saute for 2 minutes and add the red wine, water, tomato sauce, red wine vinegar and herb de provence. Stir the sauce and add the lamb shanks back to the pot. Cover and cook on a low heat for 3 hrs. Give an occasional stir every 30 minutes.

While that's being prepared, add your potatoes to a pot with water to make the mashed potatoes. Cook on a medium heat for 20 - 25 minutes until fork tender. Drain and add the potatoes back to the pot and allow them to dry out.

In a small pot, heat your cream and butter. Mash the potatoes thoroughly before adding the liquid. Add salt to your preference.

126

# Curry Chicken

*Serves:* 2-4    *Prep time:* 1.5 hr    *Total time:* 1.5 hr

---

**Soak**
1 lime
1 tbsp salt
2 cups water

**Curry Chicken**
6 boneless skinless chicken thighs cut into pieces
2 ½ tbsp curry powder
½ tsp turmeric
1 medium potato diced
1 small knob of ginger
4 cloves garlic minced
5 sprigs of thyme
1 small onion diced
1 scallion chopped up
1 small carrot
4 pimento berries (substitute with ½ tsp ground allspice)
2 tbsp olive oil

Soak the chicken in lime and salt for 30 minutes.

Rinse and drain the chicken.

Add the 1 ½ tbsp of curry powder, onion, smashed knob of ginger, potato, scallion, carrot and thyme and marinate for 30 minutes to an hour in a covered bowl.

In a large pot, add the oil and 1 tbsp curry powder and turmeric, burn the curry for 1 minute to activate the aromatics. Add the marinated chicken and potato and veggies. Stir occasionally for 2-3 minutes and then add ½ water on low for 35 minutes. Giving an occasional stir until the liquid has reduced to a thin gravy.

Serve with white rice.

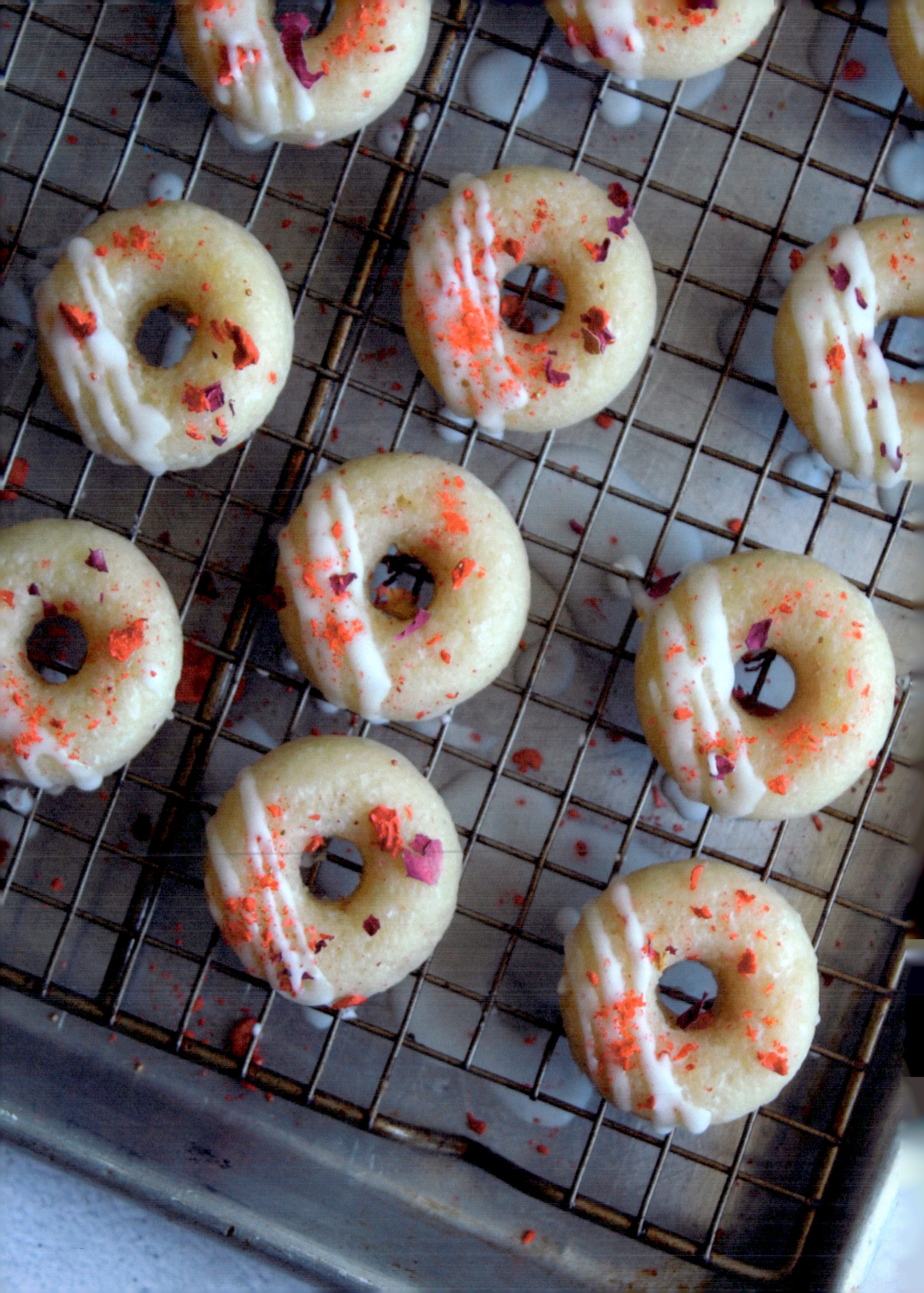

# Sweet Finale

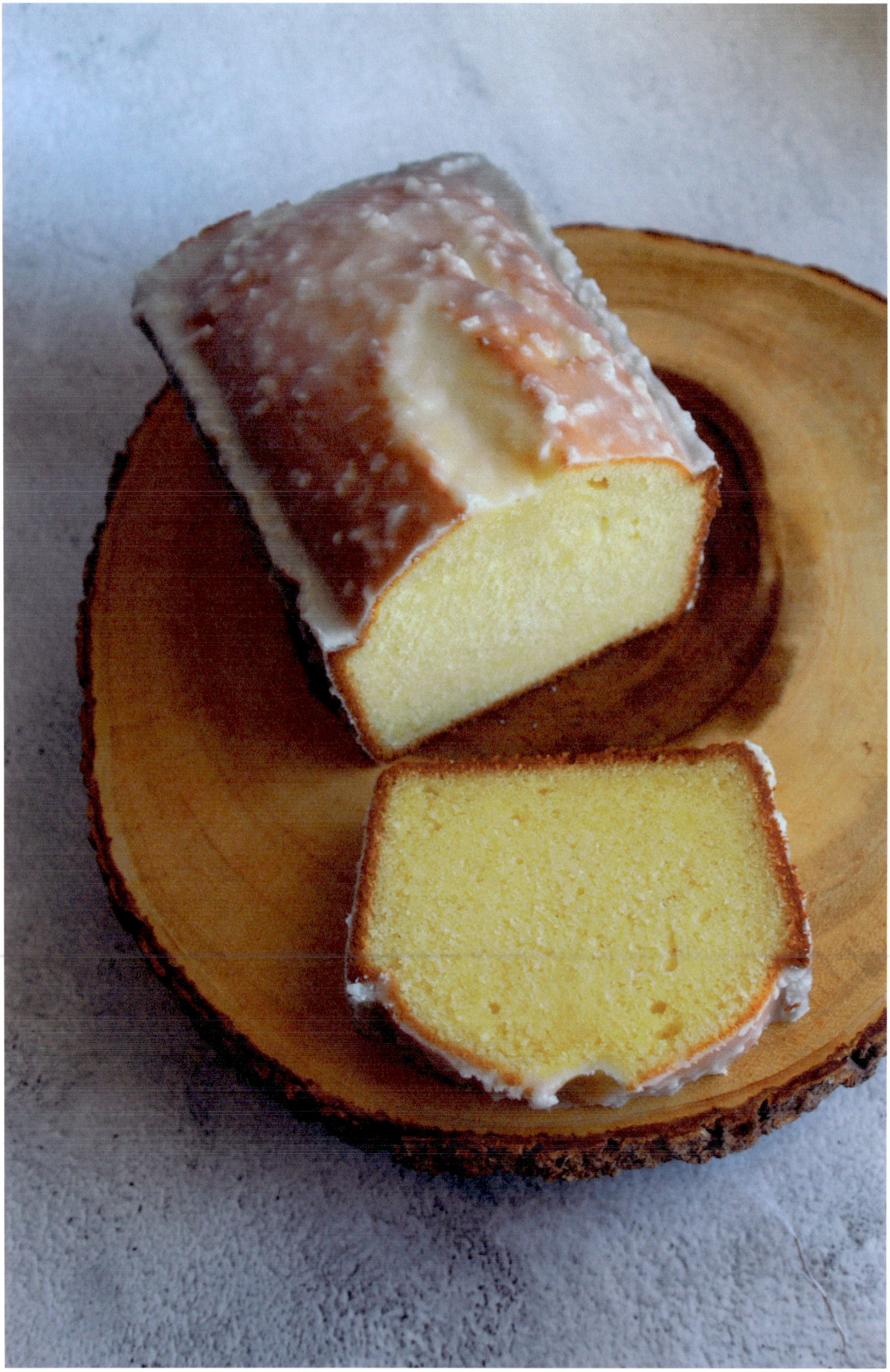

# Colleen's Pound Cake

**Serves:** 6  **Prep time:** 25 min  **Total time:** 1.5 hr

---

**Cake**
1 cup unsalted butter
1 cup sugar
1 tsp salt
1 ½ tsp vanilla
½ tsp baking powder
1 ½ cup all purpose flour
½ yogurt
4 eggs

**Glaze**
3 tbsp butter
1 cup confectioners sugar
1 tsp vanilla
1/4 cup milk
2 tbsp shredded unsweetened coconut flakes

Preheat your oven to 350 degrees. Grease the loaf pan and add flour to coat all sides and edges. Shake out any excess flour.

Cream your butter and sugar until smooth.

Add the eggs, vanilla and yogurt, beat for 1 minute to blend with the creamed butter and sugar.

Sift the dry ingredients and add to the mix slowly to incorporate. Beat for 1 more minute, this isn't a batter we want to overwork.

Place the batter into the loaf pan and place in the oven on the middle rack for 1 hour and 5 minutes.

Use a toothpick to ensure the cake is cooked. The toothpick should come out clean.

Add all ingredients for the glaze into a pot and cook for 3 minutes.

Cool the cake completely and add the glaze. The glaze will set within 20 minutes.

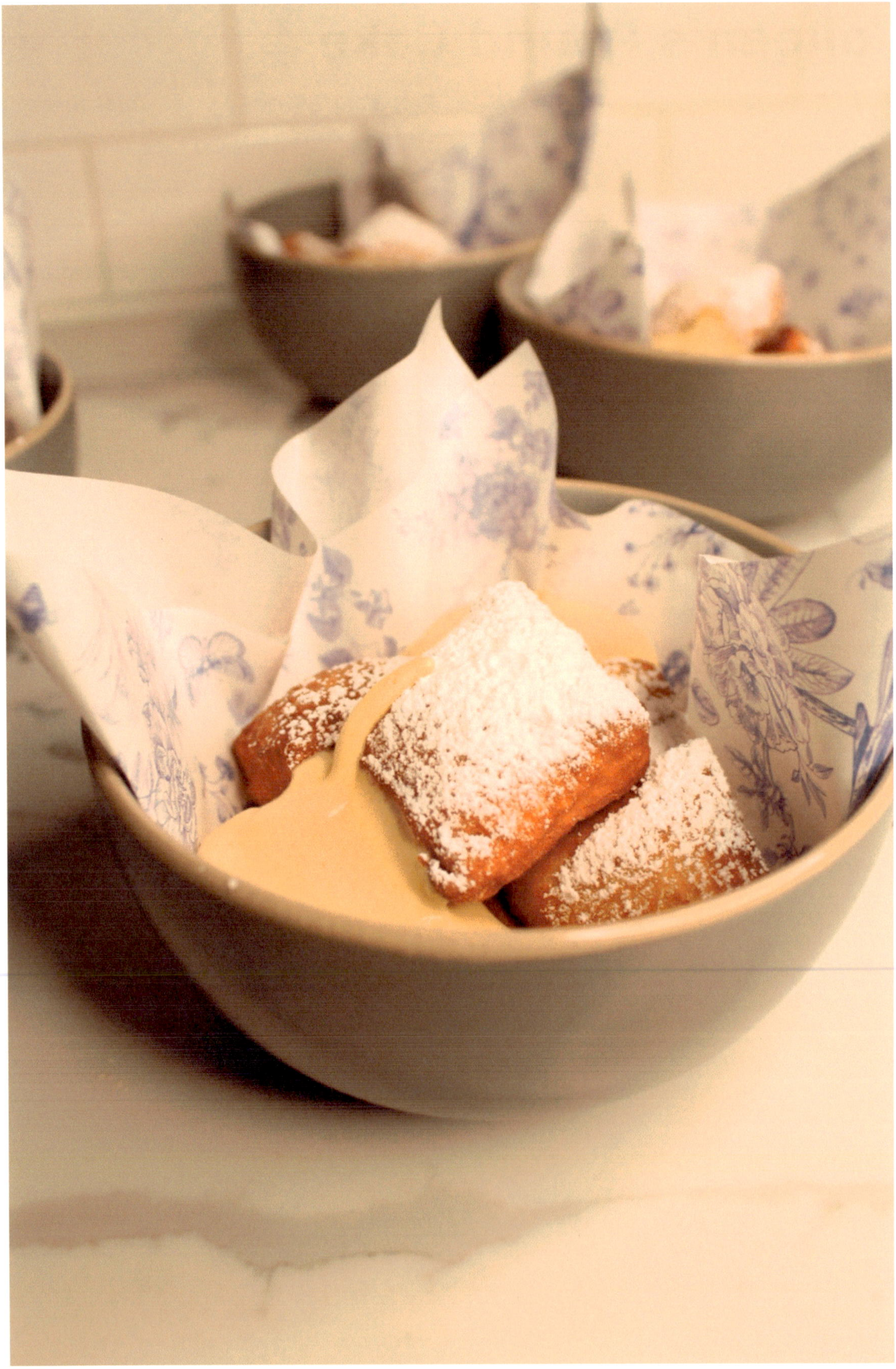

# Beignets w/ dulce de leche cream

**Serves:** 6    **Prep time:** 2 hrs    **Total time:** 2hr 20 min

---

1 ½ cups warm water
2/3 cup granulated sugar
2 large eggs (room temp)
1 cup evaporated milk
2 ¼ tsp active dry yeast
2 ½ tsp vanilla extract
7 cups bread flour
1 ½ tsp salt
5 tbsp unsalted butter (room temp)

**Dulce de leche cream**
2 cups heavy cream
1 cup powdered sugar
1 can condensed milk

Powdered sugar to finish
Vegetable oil for frying

In a small bowl, mix the water, sugar and yeast, allow the yeast to bloom and become active for 7 - 10 minutes.

Using your stand mixer with the hook attachment, add the eggs, milk, vanilla and half of the flour on a low speed for 3 minutes. Add the yeast mixture and mix slowly until incorporated, add the remaining flour and mix for 4 more minutes, add the butter and mix for an additional minute.

Cover the bowl with plastic wrap and refrigerate for 2 hrs before handling.

Generously flour your surface and rolling pin. Roll the dough out giving ½ inch thickness and cut into 1 ½ inch squares.

Heat your oil to 350 degrees and fry for 30 seconds on each side. Drain on a paper towel and sprinkle with powdered sugar.

To make the dulce de leche cream. Boil the can of condensed milk for 3 hours and let the can cool before handling.

Using a stand mixer, beat the sugar and dulce de leche until smooth. Add the heavy cream and beat until it becomes aerated and thickened for 2 minutes.

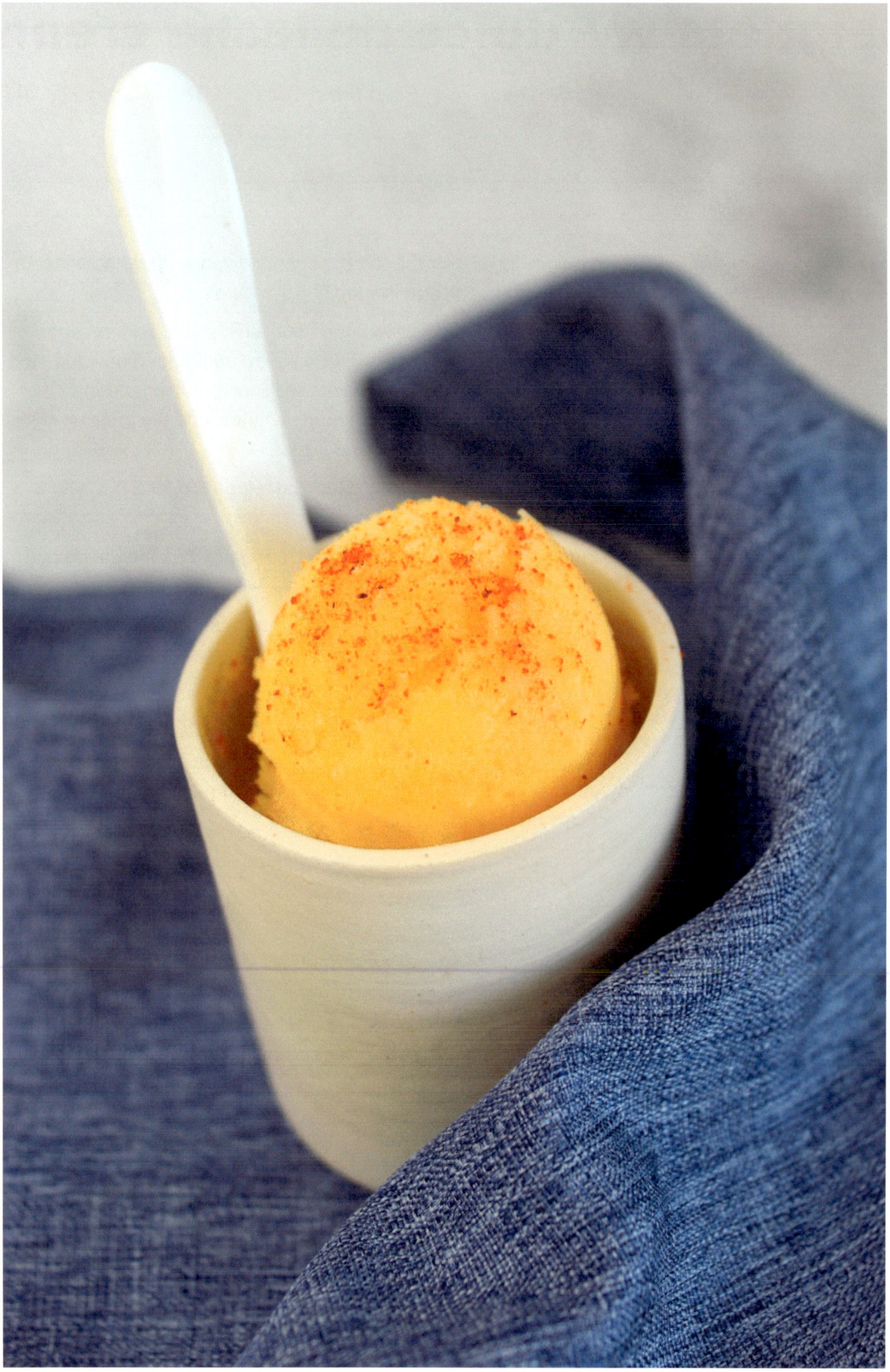

# Spiced Pineapple Mango Sorbet

*Serves:* 2-3    *Prep time:* 10 min    *Total time:* 10 min

---

1 lb peeled ripe mangoes (frozen)
1 lb diced pineapple (frozen)
1/2 cup coconut milk
4 tbsp honey
1/2 tsp cayenne pepper

Put the frozen mangoes, pineapple, honey, cayenne pepper & coconut milk in a blender and blend until smooth. Scrape the sides if necessary. Serve immediately or place in the freezer.

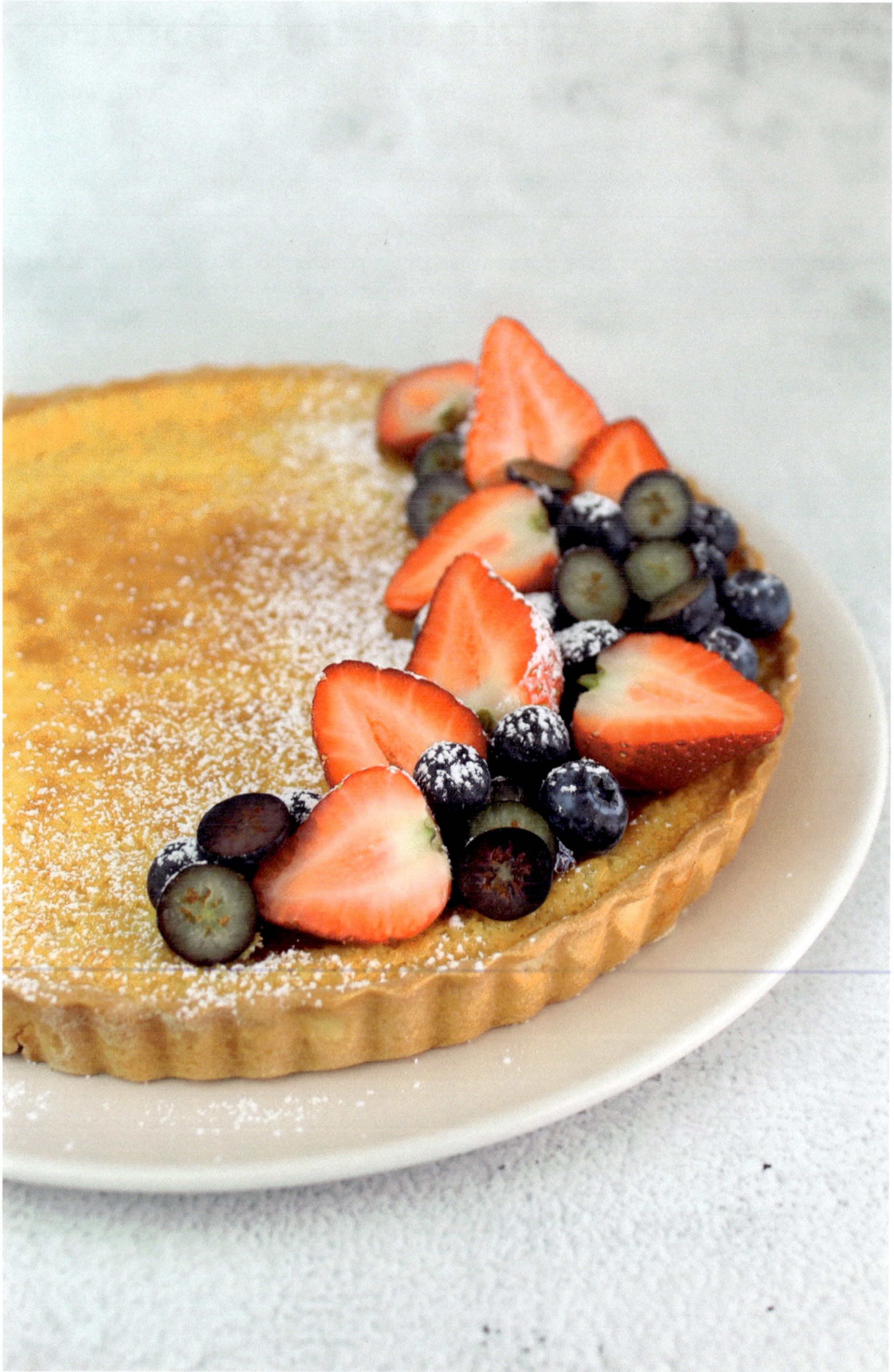

# Buttermilk Tart

**Serves:** 6  **Prep time:** 1 hr  **Total time:** 1.5 hr

---

**Dough**
1 1/2 all purpose flour
1/2 cup powdered sugar
1/2 teaspoon of salt
1 tsp vanilla extract
1 egg
8 tbsp (1 stick of butter) cubed

**Filling**
1 1/4 cup of sugar
1/2 cup room temp butter
3 tbsp all purpose flour
1/4 tsp salt
3 large eggs
1 tbsp lemon juice
1 cup buttermilk
1 tsp vanilla extract

Using a food processor combine your dry ingredients.

Add the cold butter and pulse until it resembles crumbs.

Add the egg and vanilla and continue to pulse until the dough comes together.

Turn the dough onto a floured surface and form a ball, the dough should not be sticky. Flatten the dough slightly and wrap with plastic wrap for at least 30 minutes.

Return to a lightly floured surface and roll out the dough. Place into a 9 inch tart pan using the floured rolling pin, roll the dough onto the pin and transfer to the pan. Pinch into the edges of the pan and trim with a sharp knife. Place into the fridge to firm up.

To make the filling, cream the butter and sugar.

Add flour, salt and eggs and beat until smooth.

Add the buttermilk, lemon juice and vanilla. Incorporate until fully combined.

Preheat your oven to 350 degrees.

Place the tart shell on a sheet pan and pour the mixture carefully midway as the filling tends to rise during baking. Bake for 50 minutes, allowing time to cool before serving.

Place your favorite fruit jam on the side of the pie filling and place fresh cut berries on top and dust with powdered sugar lightly.

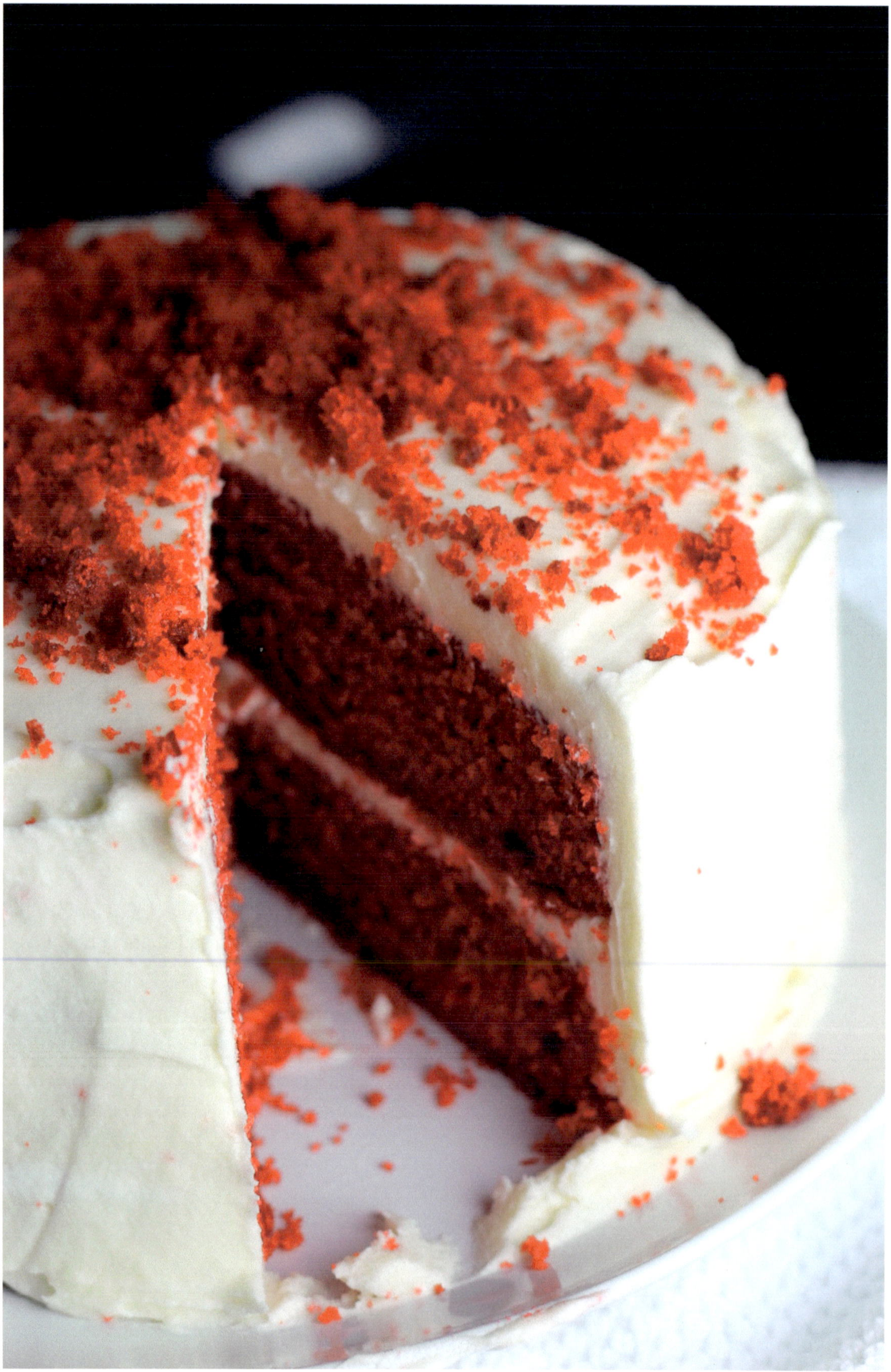

# O's Red Velvet Cake

*Serves:* 8-10   *Prep time:* 15 min   *Total time:* 3 hr

**Cake**
2 ½  cups all purpose flour
1 ½  cups of sugar
1 tsp salt
1 tsp baking soda
1 tbsp cocoa powder
1/2 cup of mini chocolate chips (fold into the cake once batter is complete) Wet ingredients
2 large eggs at room temp
1 cup buttermilk at room temp
1 1/2 cups vegetable oil

**Frosting**
1 tsp vanilla extract
1 lb softened cream cheese
4 cups powdered sugar
2 sticks unsalted butter (room temp)

Preheat the oven to 350 degrees.

In your mixing bowl, slowly combine wet ingredients.

Sift the dry ingredients and add to the mixer slowly. Mix for 2 minutes on a low to medium speed.

Prepare your baking pans by coating with butter and placing parchment paper covering the bottom of the pans.

Divide the cake batter evenly among the 2 round cake pans. Sprinkle mini chocolate chips across the top.

Place the pans in the oven evenly spaced apart. Bake for 30 minutes and insert a toothpick into the center of the cakes, when it comes out clean the cake is finished.

Allow the cake to cool, run a knife along the edge to assist in removing the cake from the pan.

Whip the butter and cream cheese until smooth, add the vanilla extract and powdered sugar, cup by cup until incorporated. Chill for 20 minutes and frost your cake.

Place the first cake layer top side down, using an offset spatula, spread some of the frosting over the top of the cake. Spread enough frosting to create a 1/4 inch layer. Carefully repeat with the following layer. Top with the remaining layer and cover the entire cake with the remaining frosting.

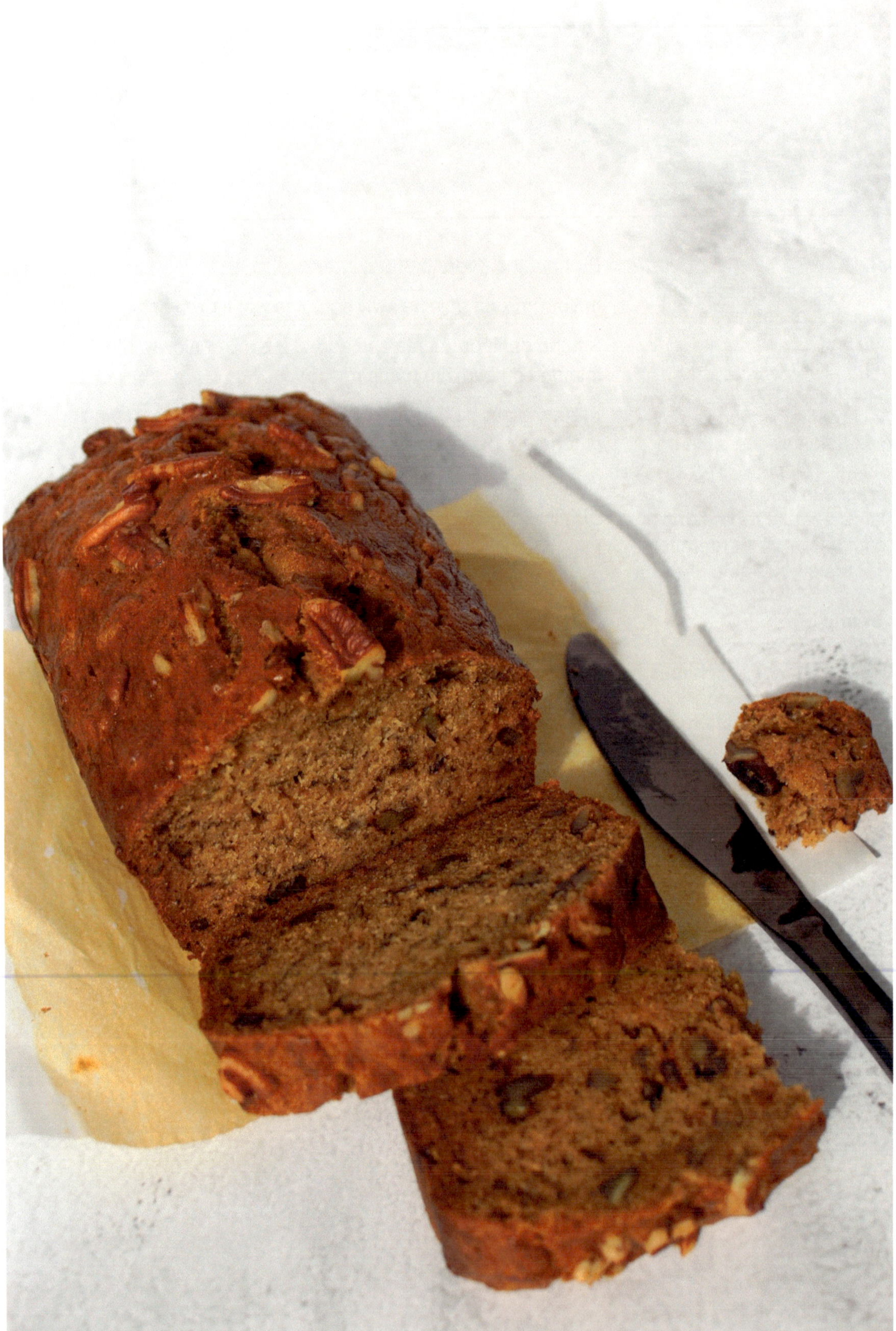

# Cam's Banana Bread

**Serves:** 6  **Prep time:** 15 min  **Total time:** 1.5 hr

---

8 tbsp (1 stick of butter softened)
2 large eggs
3 ripe bananas
1 tsp vanilla extract
2 cups of all purpose flour
3/4 cup of brown sugar
1 tsp baking soda
1 tsp cinnamon
1/2 tsp nutmeg
1/2 tsp salt
2 tbsp pancake syrup
1 cup pecan bits

Preheat your oven to 350 degrees.

Grease a loaf pan with butter and dust with a light coating of flour.

Using your mixer with the paddle attachment, mash the banana and set aside.

Cream your butter and sugar, then add the remaining wet ingredients.

Sift your dry ingredients and incorporate into the mixture bit by bit, until fully incorporated.

Add the batter to your lined baking pan and bake for 45-50 minutes. Use a toothpick or fork to test doneness. The toothpick should come out clean.

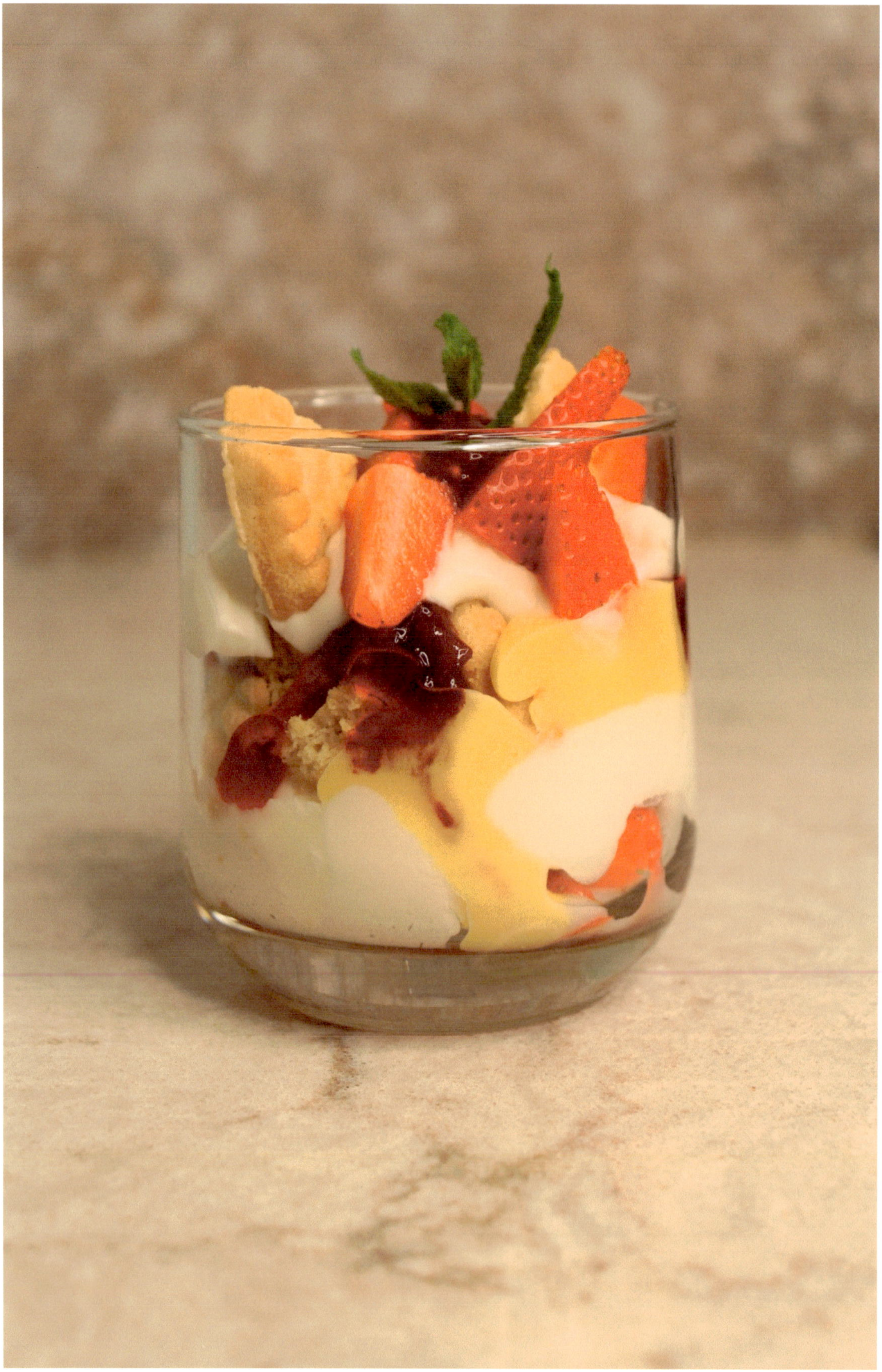

# Shortbread Cookie Trifle

*Serves:* 4  *Prep time:* 15 min  *Total time:* 20 min

---

2 cups sliced strawberries
1 pack of shortbread cookies
1 lemon
½ cup of strawberry jam

**Lemon Curd**
2 egg yolks
3/4 cup sugar
Juice of one lemon
1 tbsp butter

**Whipped Cream**
1 cup heavy cream
½ cup powdered sugar

To make the whipped cream, make sure the bowl & heavy cream are cold. Add the heavy cream and sugar to a bowl and whisk until stiff.

For the lemon curd, place the egg yolks and sugar in a bowl and mix over a double boiler. To do so, you will use a small pot, filled with water ¼ of the way and place a bowl over the pot and stir to allow the egg yolks to stiffen. Add the lemon juice, whisk and remove from the heat and whisk in the butter. Allow to cool fully.

To assemble the trifle. Add a layer of strawberries, jam, cookies, lemon curd & whipped cream to fill the glass.. Garnish with a mint leaf

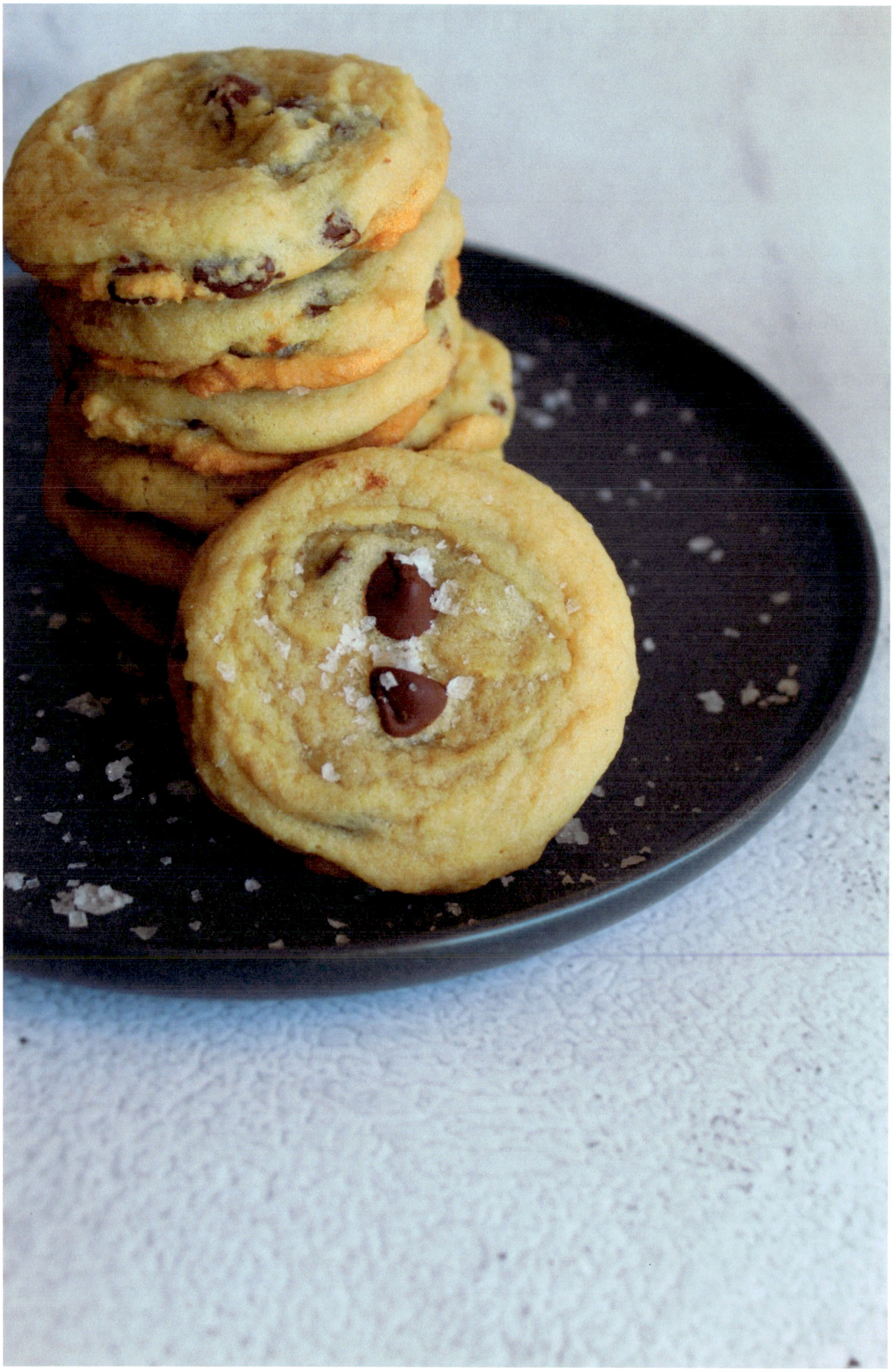

# Sea Salt Chocolate Chip Cookies

**Serves:** 10  **Prep time:** 15 min  **Total time:** 1.5 hr

---

1 cup of unsalted butter softened
1/2 cup granulated sugar
1 cup of light brown sugar tightly packed
2 large eggs, room temperature
2 tsp of vanilla extract
3 cups of all purpose flour
1 tsp of baking soda
1 tsp salt
2 cups of semi sweet chocolate chips 3/4 of the chocolate chips will be used in the mix, some will be reserved for placement on the top

In your mixer, cream the butter and sugar.

Add the eggs and vanilla extract. Using a spatula scrape the sides as needed.

Sift your dry ingredients and add to the creamed butter and sugar bit by bit until fully combined. Add the chocolate chips last.

Portion into equal size scoops, strategically place a few chips on each cookie and sprinkle the sea salt flakes lightly. Refrigerate for an additional 30 minutes.

Preheat the oven to 350 degrees and bake for 12 minutes.

Set your timer for 6 minutes and rotate your tray in the oven for even cooking. The aroma in the house is amazing, don't be compelled to fuss with the cookies, let them cool and enjoy.

Depending on the size of your scooper, this will make 24 - 36 cookies.

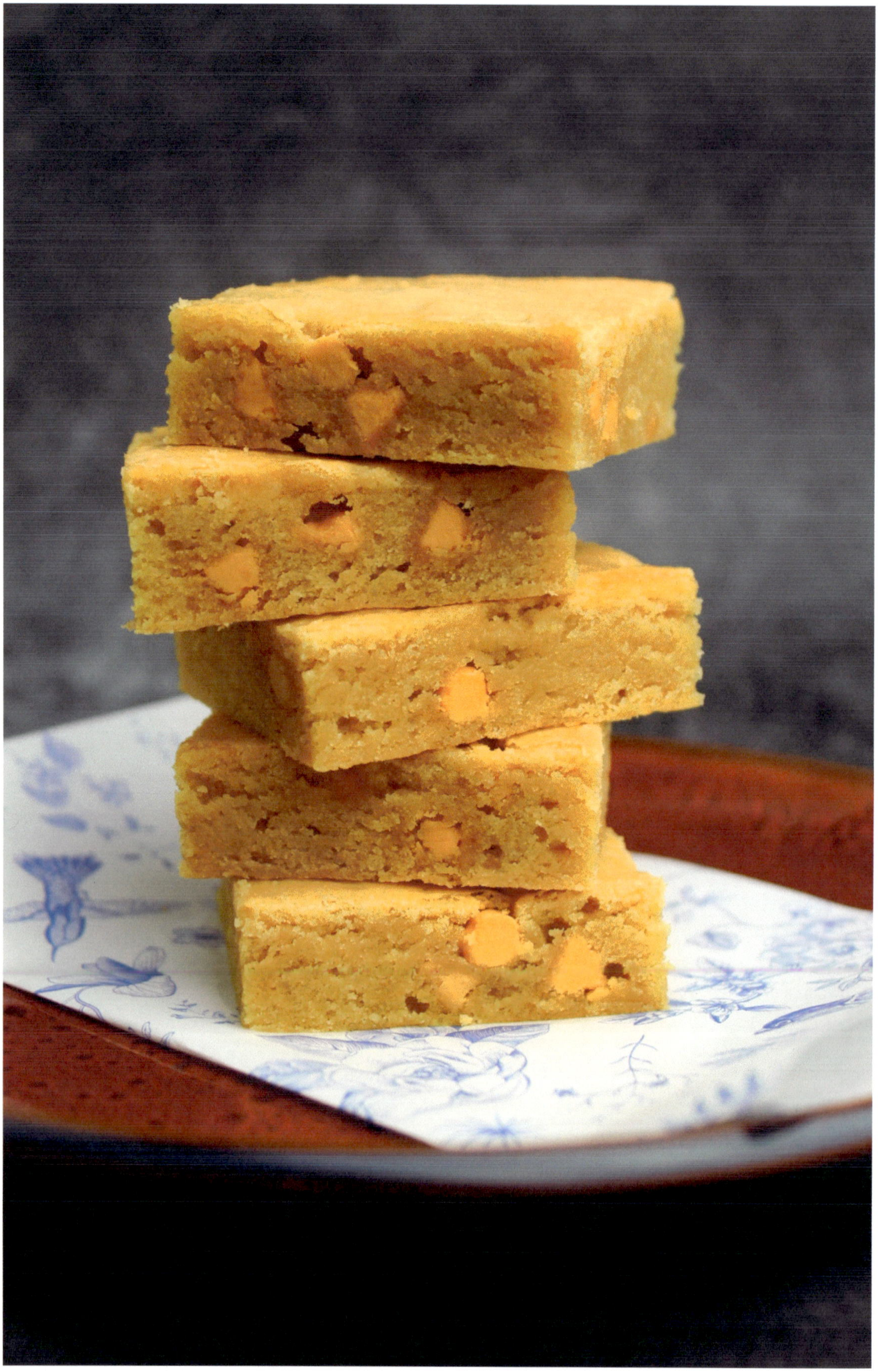

# The Cookie House Blondies

**Serves:** 10   **Prep time:** 20 min   **Total time:** 50 min

---

4 tbsp milk
1 cup butter
½ cup sugar
1 ⅓ cup brown sugar
3 eggs (room temp)
1 ½ tsp vanilla extract
2 ¼ cup AP flour
1 ½ tsp cornstarch
½ tsp baking powder
1 tsp salt
½ cup butterscotch chips

Preheat the oven to 350 degrees. Grease a 13 x 9 inch baking pan and line with parchment paper.

Brown the butter slightly in a saucepan. Strain the butter to avoid getting the brown bits in the sugar. Allow to cool for 5 minutes before adding the eggs.

Stir in the eggs and vanilla.

Mix your dry ingredients before adding to the wet ingredients.

Add the butterscotch chips and spread the blondie mix in the lined baking pan and bake for 20 minutes.

Cool, cut into squares and enjoy.

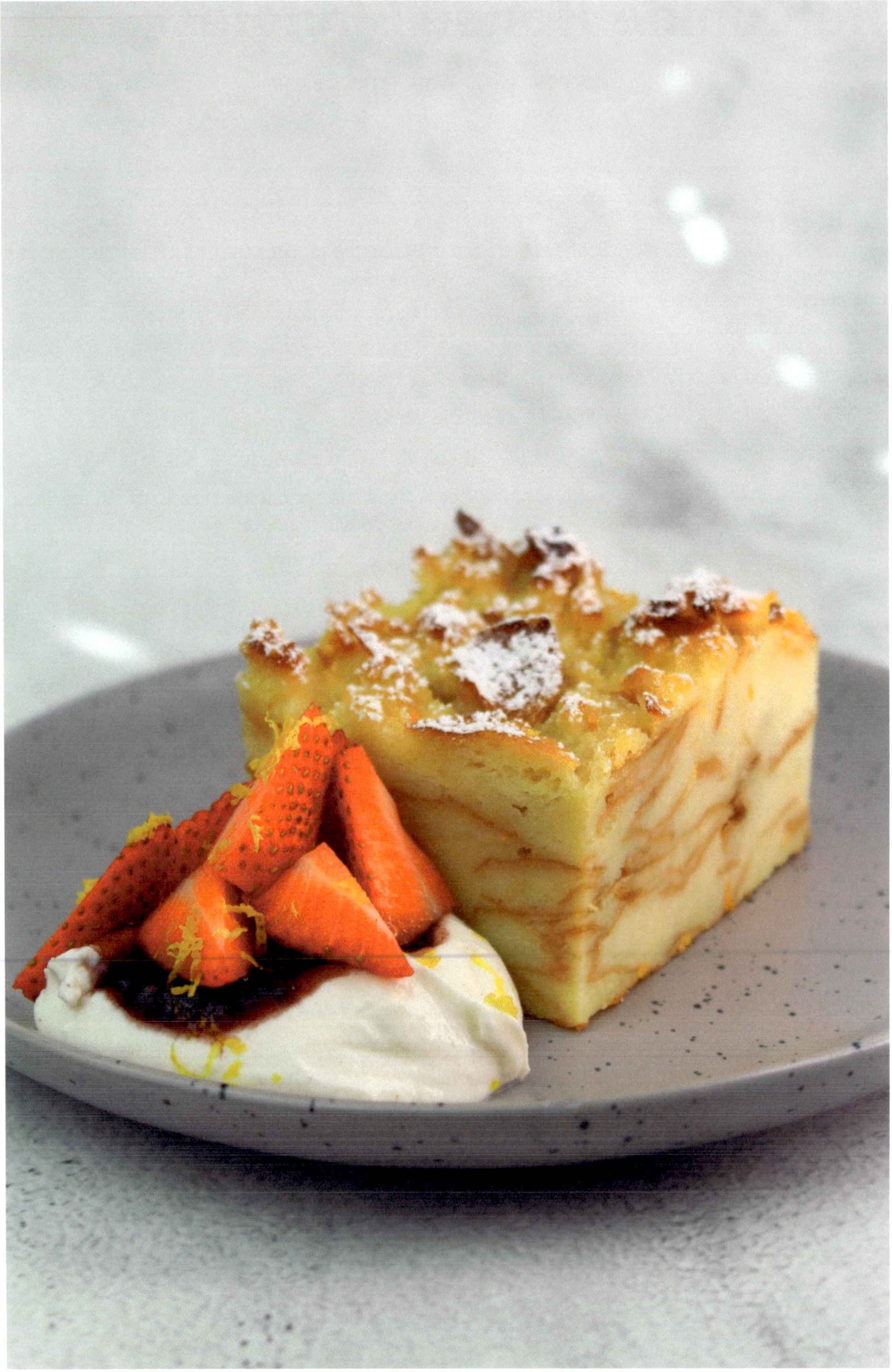

# Bread pudding w/ Chantilly Cream

***Serves:*** *6*  ***Prep time:*** *25 min*  ***Total time:*** *1.5 hr*

---

**Bread Pudding**
1 brioche loaf cut into 1 inch cubes
½ sugar
1 tsp vanilla
Zest of 1 orange
2 eggs
2 cups milk
½ cup cream

**Chantilly Cream**
2 cups of cold whipping cream
1/2 cup powdered sugar
1 tsp vanilla extract
1 tsp Gran marnier

Preheat your oven to 350 degrees.

Using a large bowl add the brioche.

Mix the wet ingredients, zest and sugar. Pour over the bread and mix.

Place in a parchment line baking dish.

Bake for 40 minutes and allow to cool for 15 minutes before handling.

In a clean, cold mixing bowl, add all ingredients for the chantilly cream and whip on mid to high speed till stiff peaks begin to form.

Cut the bread pudding, add the whipped cream and optional fresh berries.

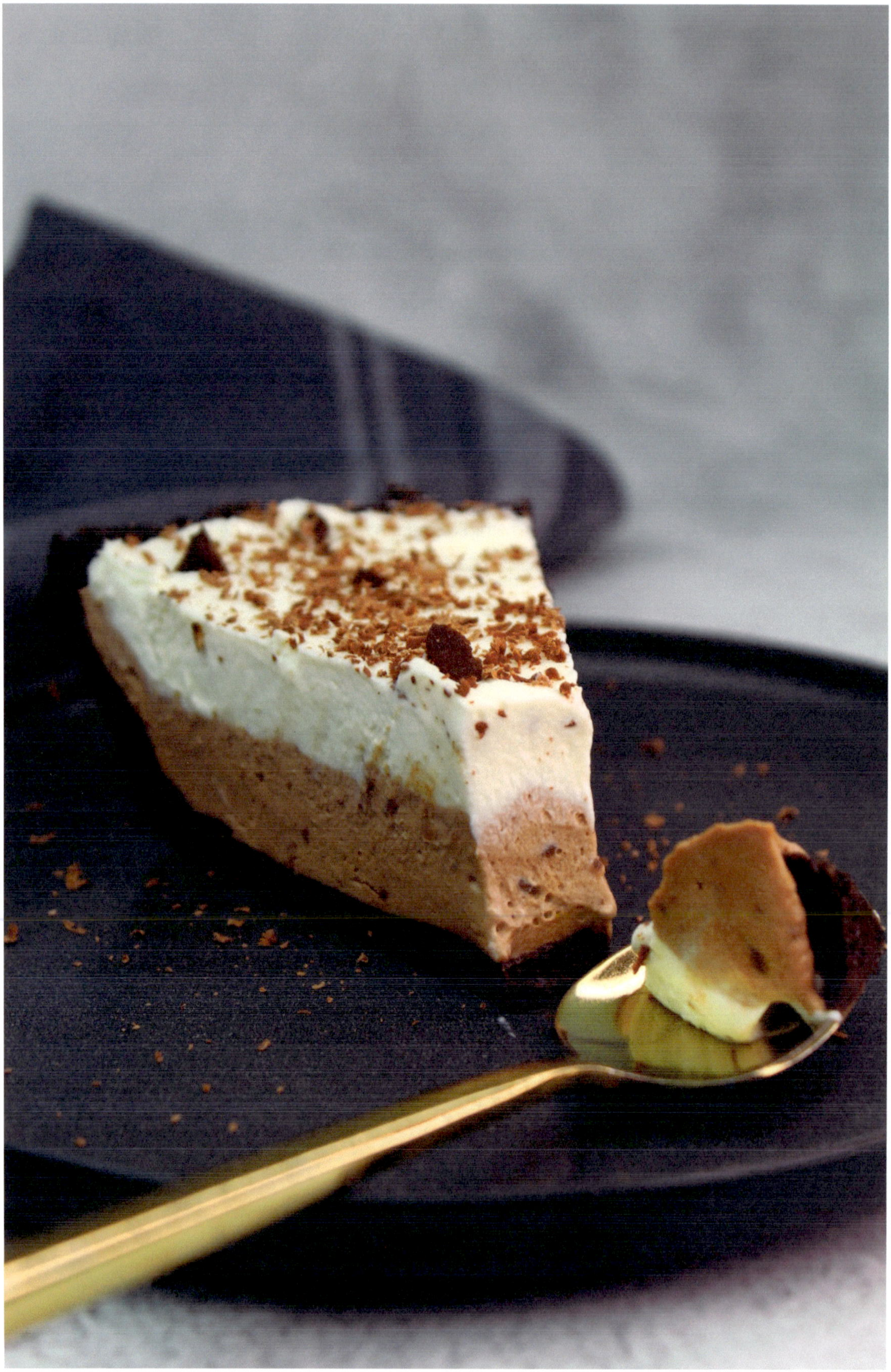

# Kissed by Coco

**Serves:** *6 - 8* **Prep time:** *20 min*  **Total time:** *2 hrs*

---

24 Oreos
8 oz cream cheese room temp
3 tbsp condensed milk
1 ¾ cup heavy cream
½ cup chocolate chips
2 oz Disaronno Liqueur
1 tsp vanilla

Using a food processor, pulse the oreos until a fine crumb is created.

Add the cream cheese and pulse until the mix forms a ball.

Using a springform pan, mold the mix evenly to the shape of the pan.

Melt the chocolate with the condensed milk. Once cooled, add 1 cup heavy cream and whip until stiff.

In a clean cold mixing bowl, whip the ¾ cup heavy cream and Disaronno until stiff.

Using an offset spatula, layer the whipped chocolate and smooth out, then layer the Disaronno whipped cream and smooth out.

Place the finished pie in the freezer for 2 hours, cut and serve. Keep the remaining pie in the fridge as this is an icebox cake.

(Friendly tip, run your knife in hot water for a clean cut.)

Mexican brownie w/ popcorn whipped cream, miso caramel mousse, crispy chocolate black rice

# Libations

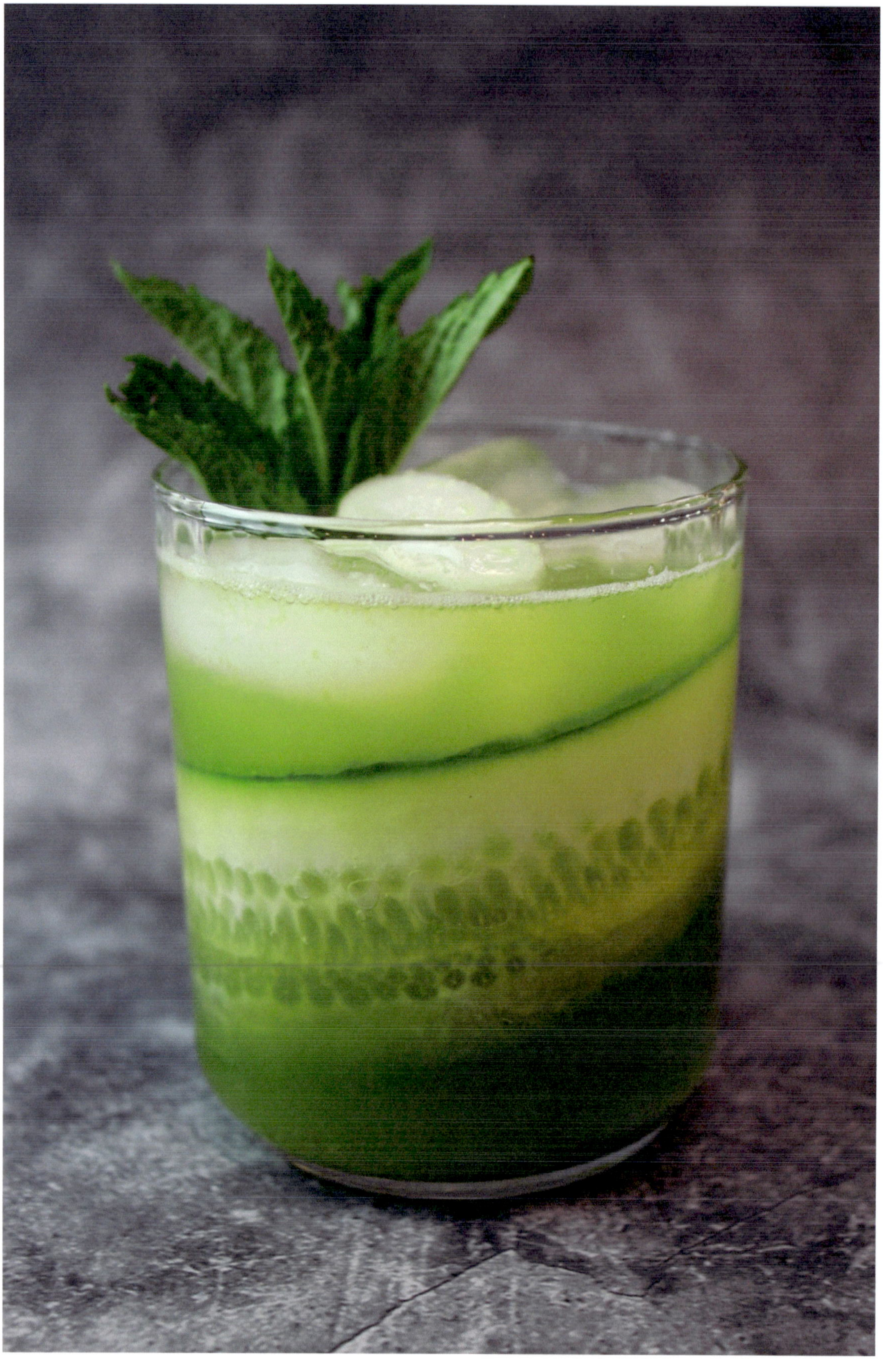

# The Doctor's Orders

**Serves:** 1   **Prep time:** 10 min   **Total time:** 10 min

---

1.5 oz Vodka
½ apple
1 celery stick
1 tbsp parsley
2 tbsp agave
3 mint leaves
¼ cucumber
¼ cup water
1 ½ lemon peeled

Add all ingredients except the vodka into a blender and strain.

In a chilled glass, line a thin slice of cucumber along the side and add ice.

Pour the vodka into the glass followed by the juice mix.

156

# The East Hampton Paloma

**Serves:** 1  **Prep time:** 5 min  **Total time:** 5 min

---

1.5 oz ElderFlower liqueur
2 oz grapefruit juice
1.5 Mezcal
¼ once simple syrup
Seltzer to top

In a shaker, add the elderflower, simple syrup, mezcal and grapefruit juice with ice. Give a vigorous shake for 20 - 30 seconds and pour over ice. Top with seltzer.

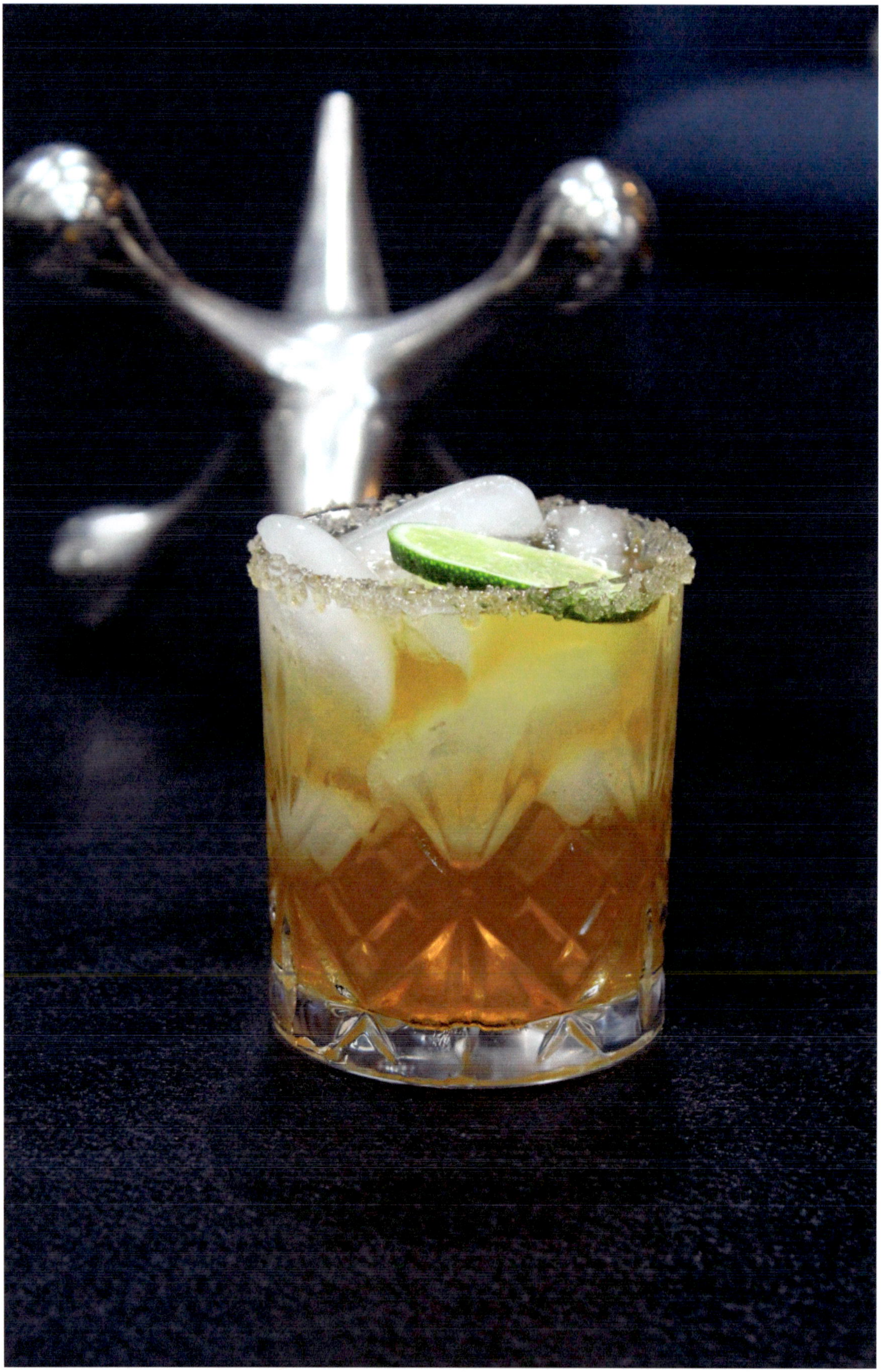

# Tamarind Elderflower Margarita

**Serves:** 1  **Prep time:** 30  **Total time:** 15 min

---

2 oz Tamarind Juice
2 oz Tequila
1 oz Ginger Syrup
1 oz Elderflower
Juice of half a lime

**Ginger Syrup**
1 cup of water
1 cup sugar
gracious stem of ginger (skin on)

**Tamarind Juice**
1/2 cup tamarind pulp w/ seeds
2 quarts water
1 cup brown sugar

Boil the water, tamarind pulp and sugar for 20 minutes.

Allow to cool slightly before straining.

To make the ginger syrup, blend the water and sugar and ginger, then boil for 5 minutes and strain.

Add all of the ingredients for the cocktail in a shake over ice. Give a vigorous shake and pour over ice.

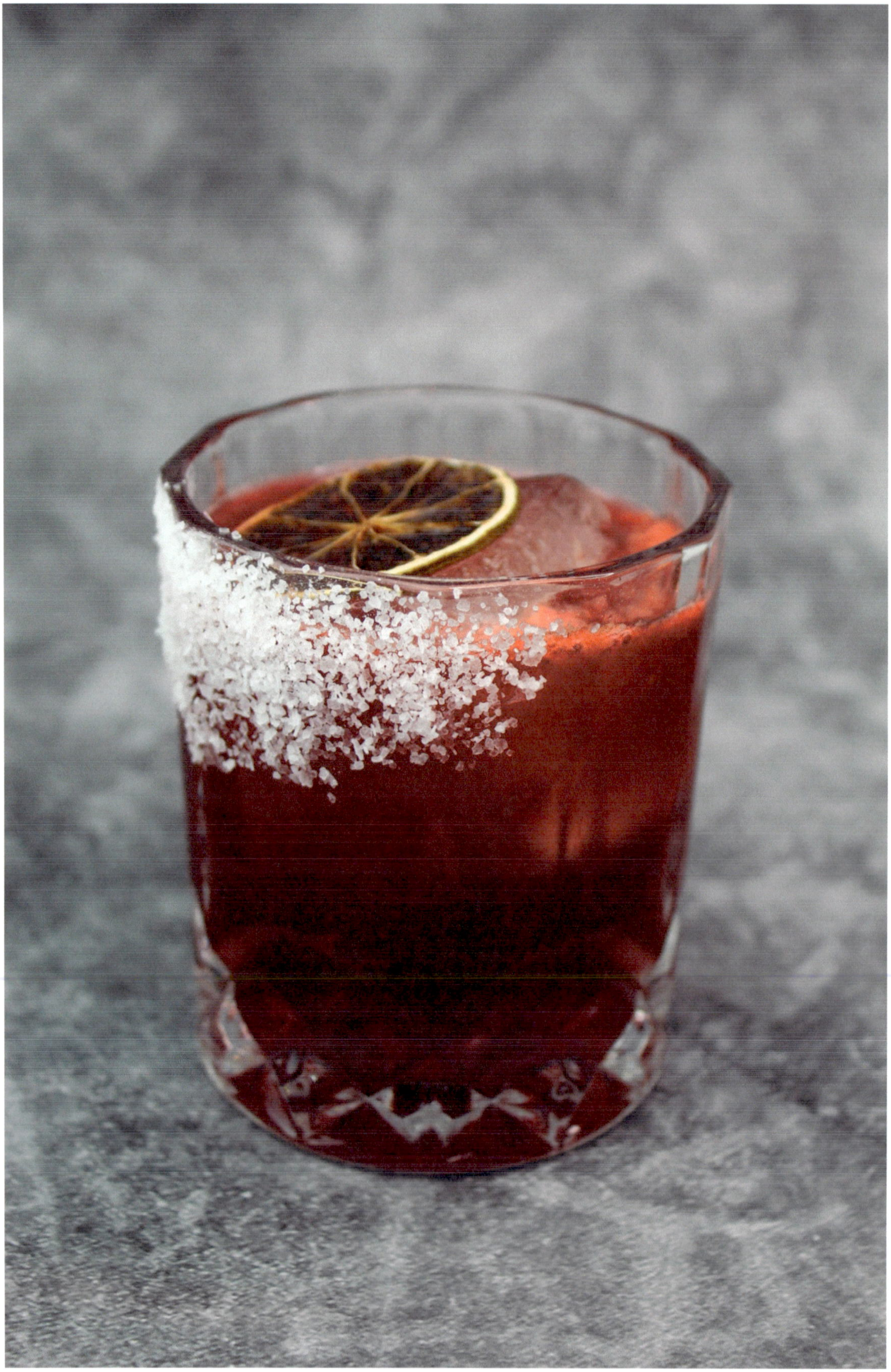

# Sorrel Margarita

**Serves:** 1  **Prep time:** 5 min  **Total time:** 5 min

2 oz sorrel
1 oz Grand Marnier
1 oz fresh lime juice
1.5 tequila
Kosher salt for the rim

**Sorrel (make ahead)**
5 cups of water
1 cup of dried sorrel (this can be found in your local west indian market)
2 cinnamon sticks
2 pcs star anise
1/2 cup of sugar (I prefer my sorrel on the sweeter side, so I add more)
1 knob of ginger smashed

Add the sorrel, Grand Marnier, lime juice and tequila to a shaker and shake vigorously for 20 seconds.

Pour over ice and enjoy.

To make the sorrel add the dried sorrel, cinnamon, ginger, star anise, water to a large pot and boil for 15 minutes. Strain, add the sugar and let cool before place in the fridge.

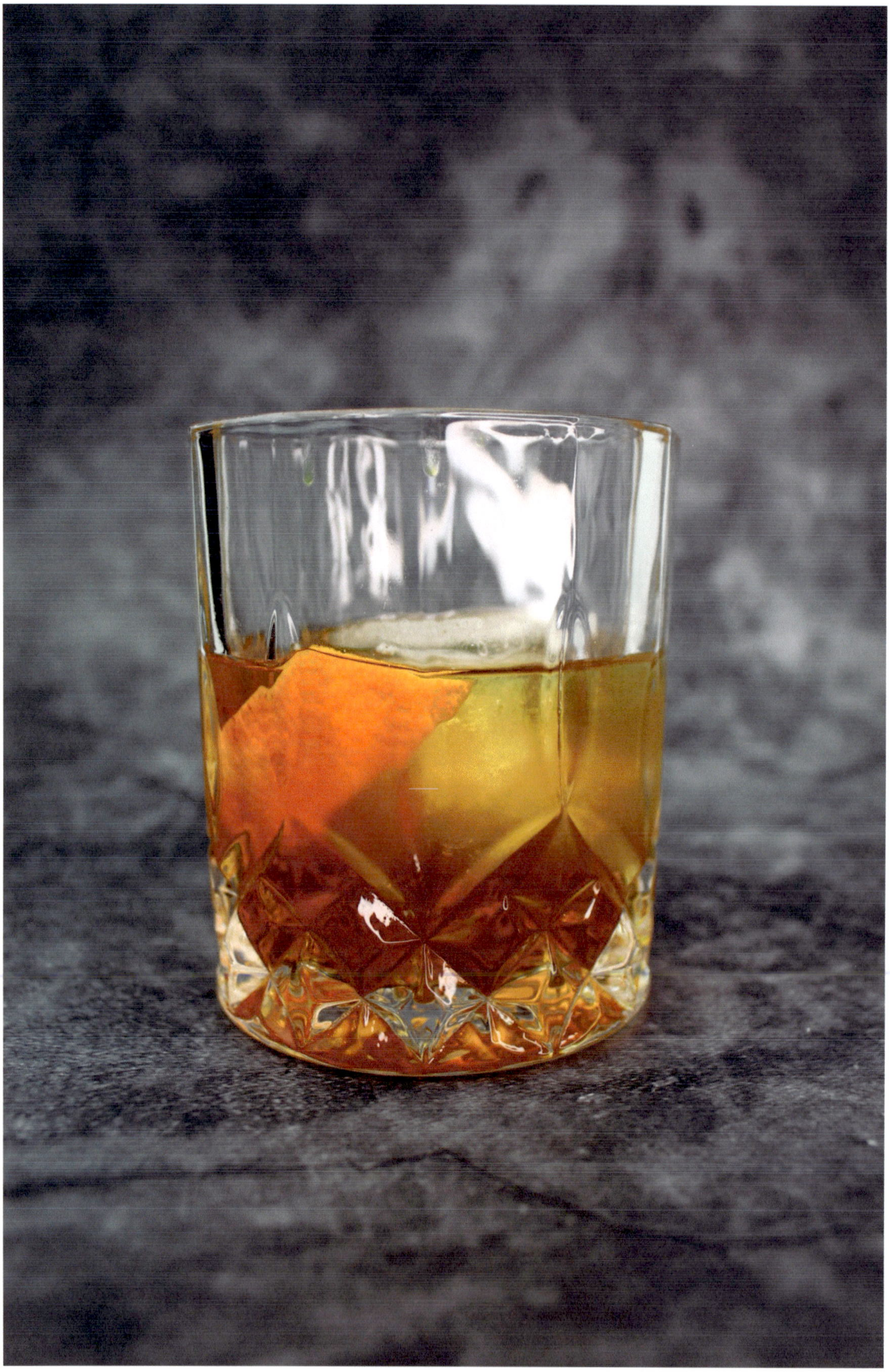

# Basil Old Fashioned

*Serves:* 1  *Prep time:* 10 min  *Total time:* 10 min

---

2 ounces Bourbon
1-2 Luxardo cherries
1 oz basil syrup
Few dashes of Angostura bitters
1 tsp water

**Basil syrup**
5 bruised basil leaves
4 tbsp sugar
½ cup water

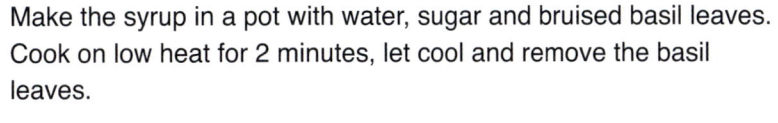

Make the syrup in a pot with water, sugar and bruised basil leaves. Cook on low heat for 2 minutes, let cool and remove the basil leaves.

The syrup can be reserved in ice cube form to extend the life.

Stir the bourbon, basil syrup, Angostura, and water together in a glass with ice.

In a rocks glass add your cubed ice, the cherries and pour the cocktail into the glass.

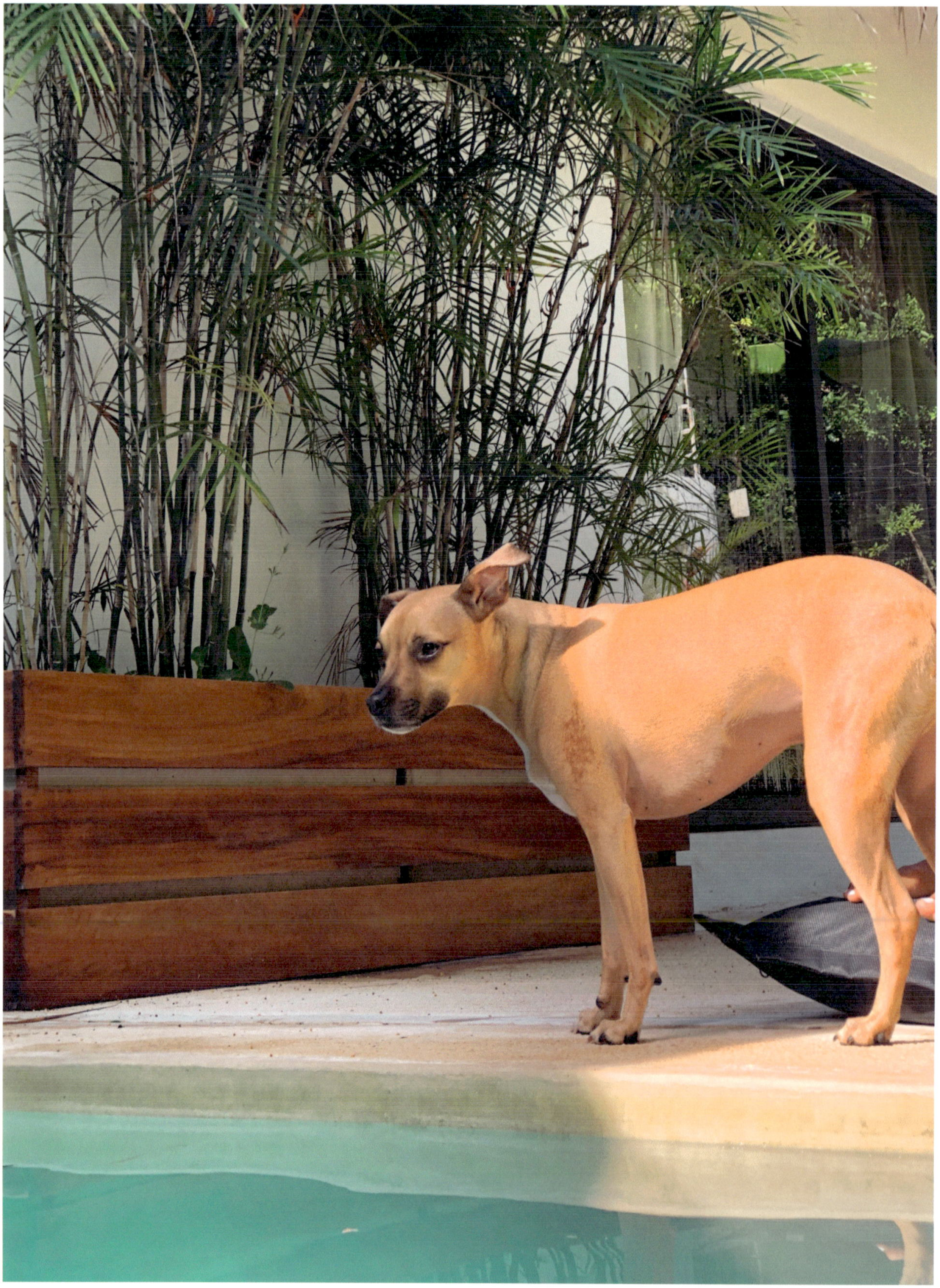

**BLEU**

CHIEF FUR BABY
FLAVOR OFFICER

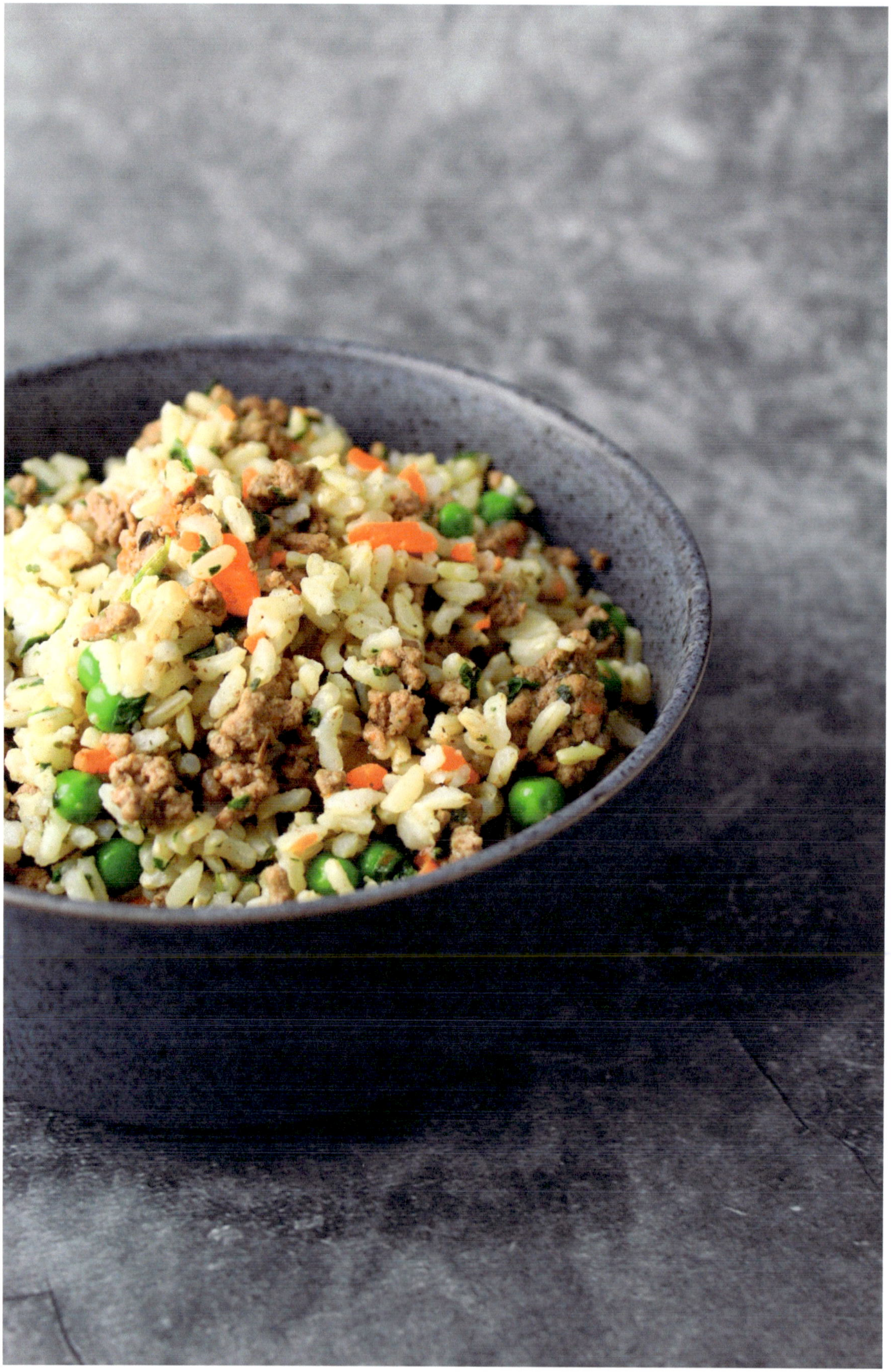

# Bleu's Dinner

**Serves:** 1 - 2 hungry pups     **Prep time:** 1hr     **Total time:** 2 hr

---

4.5 cups brown rice
12.5 cups water
3 lbs lean ground beef
1 ½ tbsp italian seasoning
½ tsp cinnamon
5 oz pack spinach
1 large carrot peeled
1 cup frozen peas
2 tbsp fresh parsley chopped finely

Rinse the rice and strain.

In a large pot, add the rice and water. Cook for 30 minutes, until tender.

Using a large pot, cook the ground beef for 6 - 8 minutes until fully cooked.

Use a food processor to chop the carrots and spinach.

Mix the carrots, spinach, peas, herbs, cinnamon, rice and beef together.

Let it cool, divide into preferred freezer safe containers and store for use throughout the week.

Friendly tip, thaw in the fridge the night before so your hungry pup doesn't throw a fit the next morning.

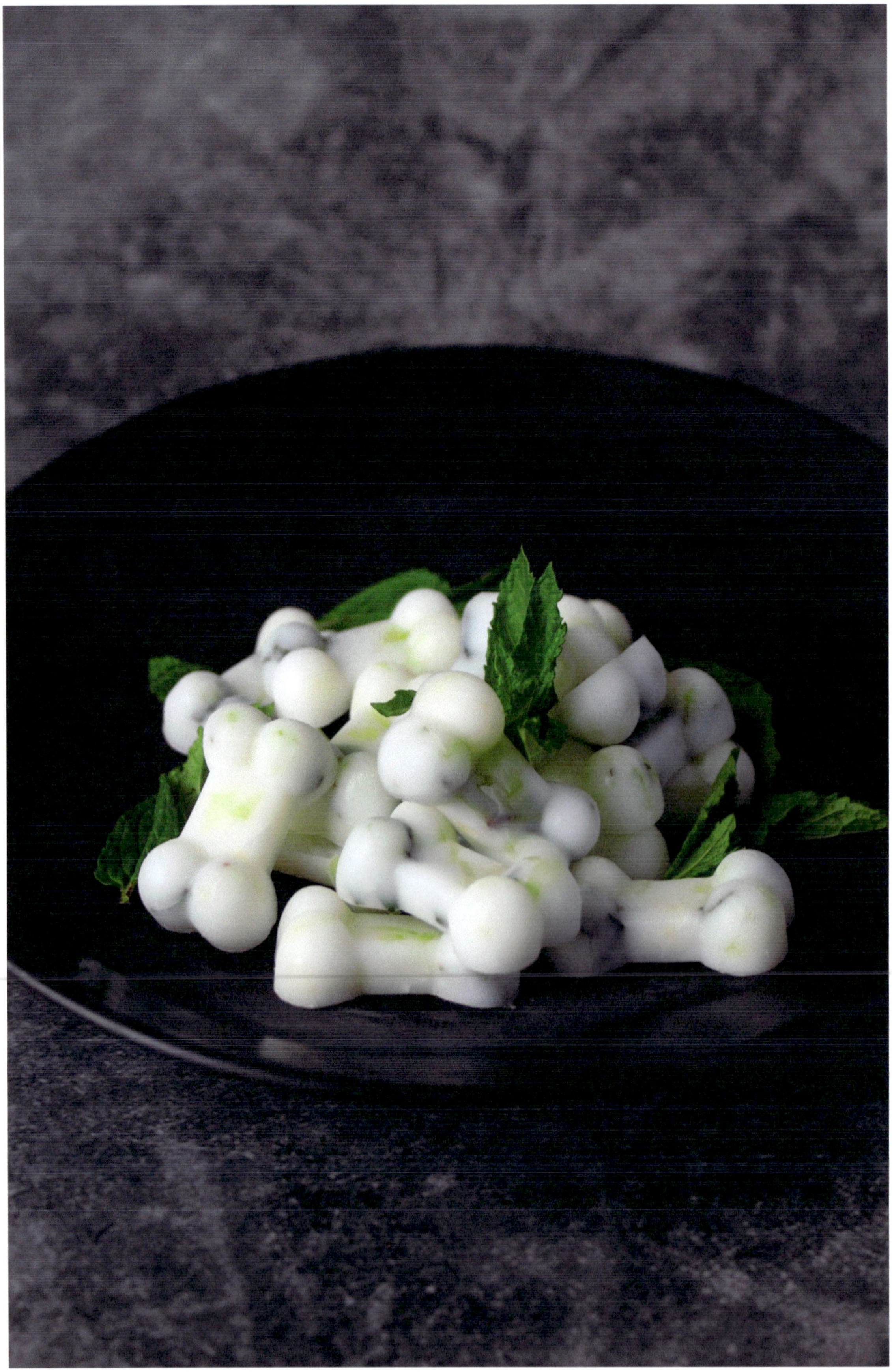

# The Breath Mint

**Serves:** 1 pup w/ stinky breath    **Prep time:** 15 min    **Total time:** 1.5 hr

---

1 ½ tbsp celery finely chopped
1 ½ tbsp green apple finely chopped
¾ cup coconut oil
7 leaves of mint torn into pieces

Heat the coconut oil for 1 minute until completely melted.

Using bone shaped silicone molds, distribute the green apple, mint and celery evenly. Pour the coconut oil into the molds and place in the freezer for an hour.

Once frozen, throw into a ziploc bag and retain in the freezer until it's time to give your pup a refreshing treat.

Gluten Free

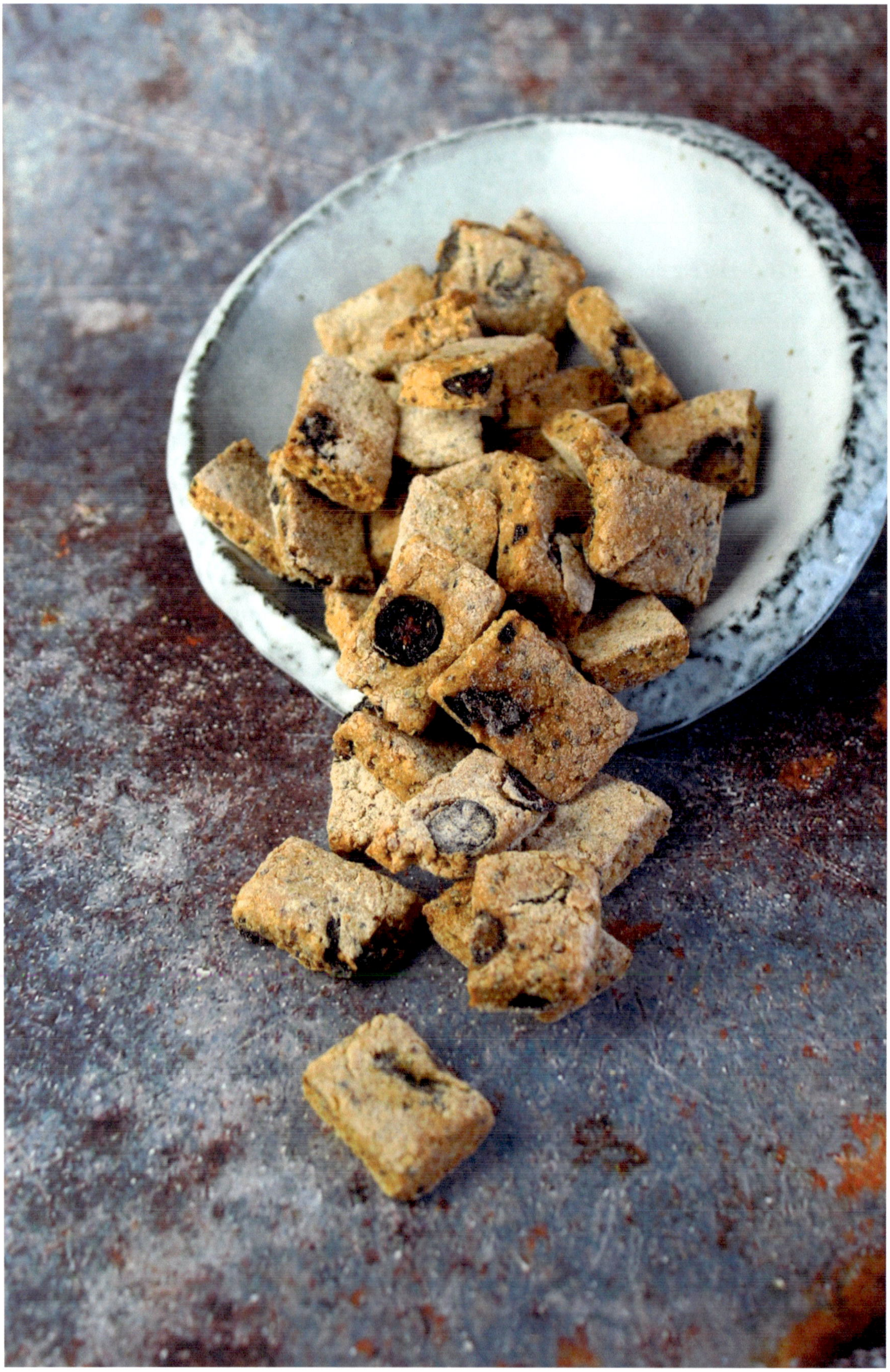

# Quinoa Blueberry Cookies

**Serves:** *1 furbaby and friends*   **Prep time:** *45 min*   **Total time:** *1 hr*

---

½ cup cold cooked quinoa
1 cup wholewheat flour
½ cup blueberries
2 eggs

In a bowl beat the eggs, add the blueberries, quinoa and wheat flour. Mix the ingredients with a spatula, this will create a stiff dough.

Flour your surface and rolling pin, roll out the dough and cut into 1 inch squares.

Place on a parchment lined baking sheet and bake for 25 minutes at 350 degrees.

Let the cookies cool and store in an airtight container for 5- 6 days.

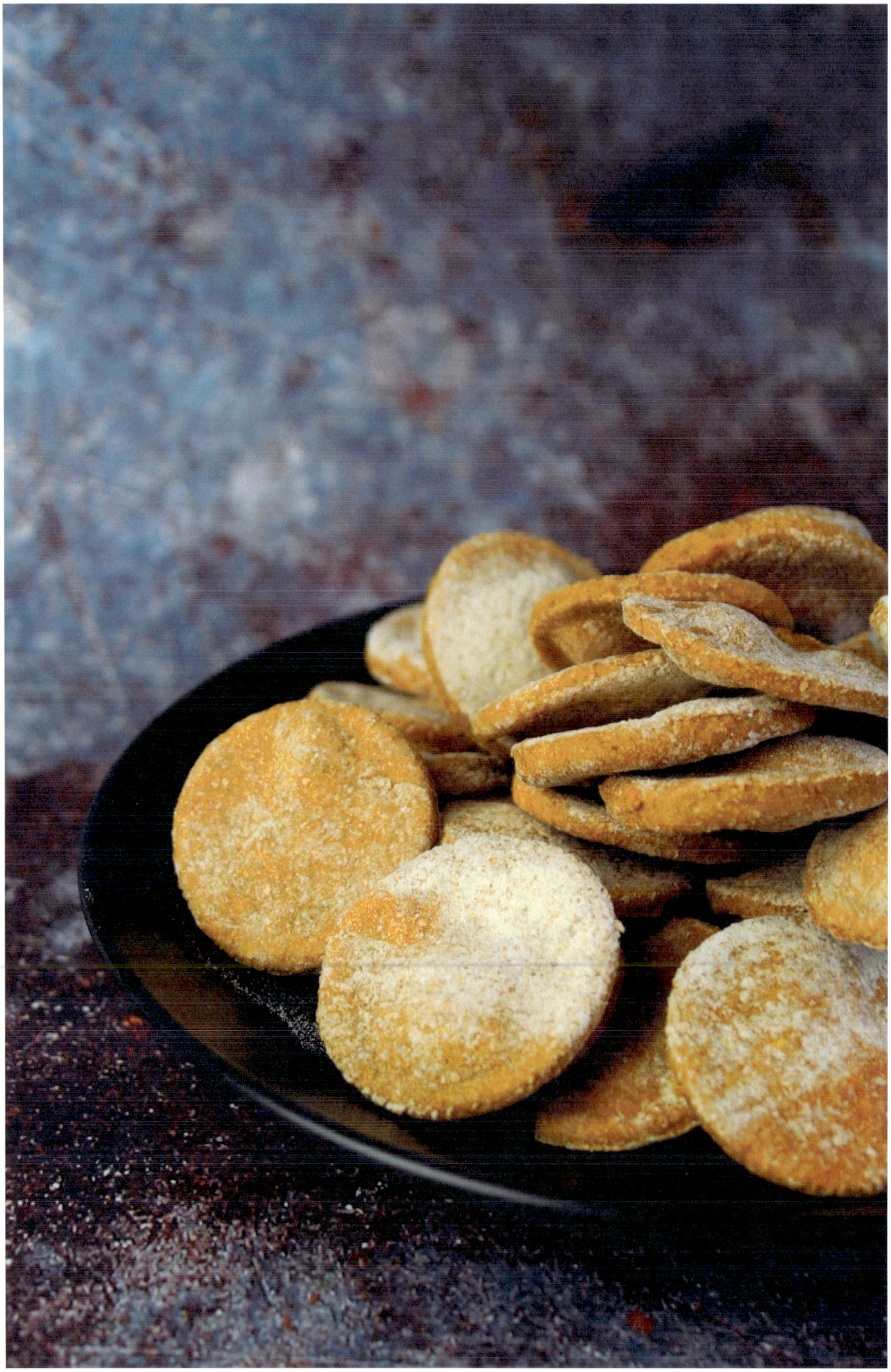

# Sweet Potato Cracker

**Serves:** 1 hungry pup & friends  **Prep time:** 1 hr  **Total time:** 1 hr

---

1 medium sweet potato
2 eggs
2 ½ cups of wheat flour

Roast the sweet potato for 25 minutes at 350 degrees.

Once the sweet potato has cooled a bit, add to a food processor with the flour and eggs. Pulse until a dough forms.

Flour your work surface and rolling pin, roll the dough out very thin, and use a cookie cutter to cut the dough.

Place onto a parchment lined baking sheet and bake at 350 degrees for 25 minutes.

Let the crackers cool and store in an airtight container for up to a week.

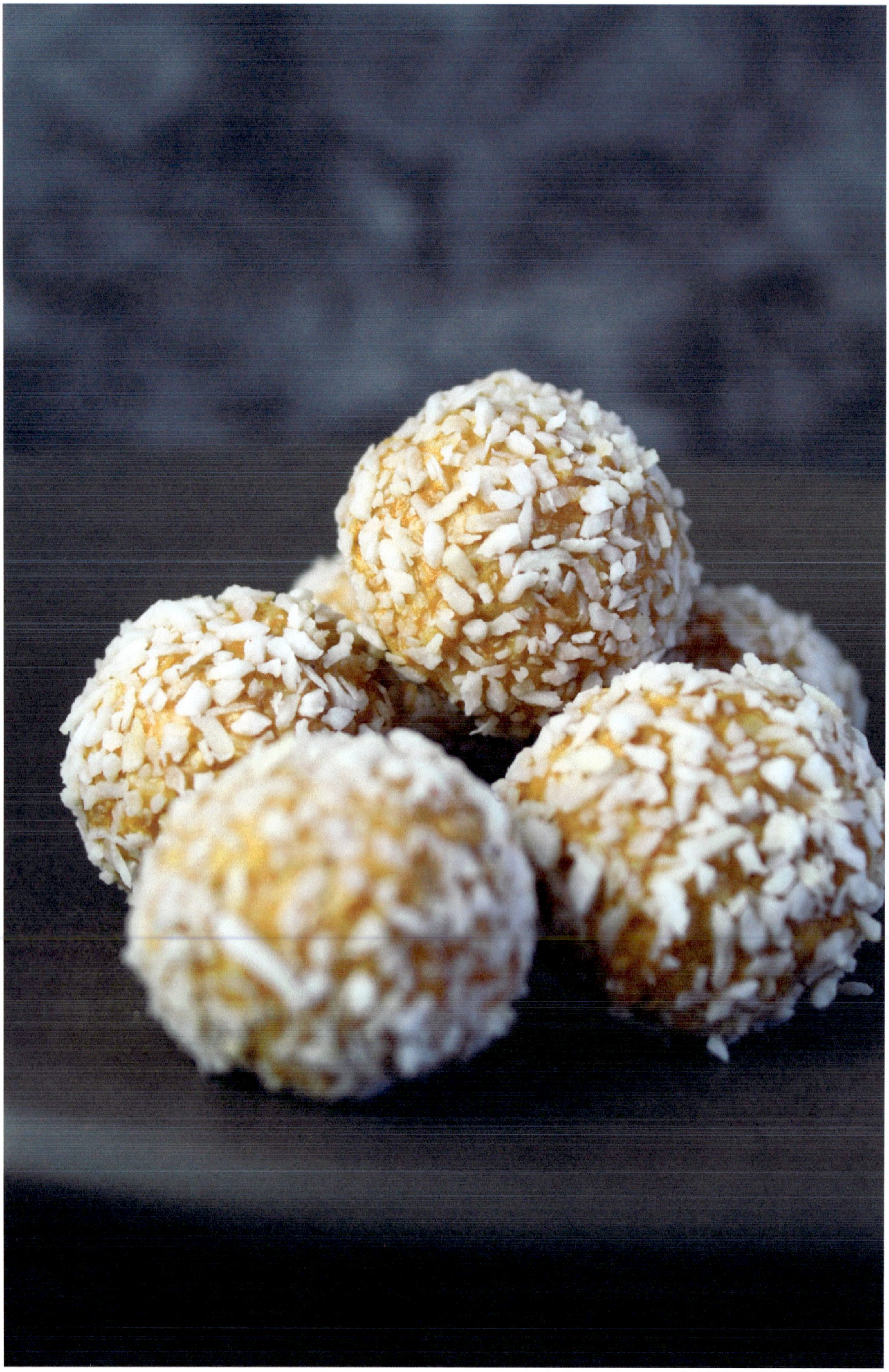

# Peanut Buddy Oat Bites

**Serves:** 1 fur baby   **Prep time:** 15 min   **Total time:** 35 min

---

½ cup rolled oats
½ cup unsweetened coconut flakes
1 tbsp honey
½ tsp cinnamon
½ cup peanut butter

Mix all of the ingredients together in a bowl and evenly divide into small balls.

Roll in shredded coconut and keep in the fridge for up to 2 weeks in an airtight container.

*Gluten Free*

Photo Credit: Brian Jamie

# ACKNOWLEDGEMENTS

To my mum and dad, thank you for being there through every step, every idea and every concept I've brought to life. More importantly, thank you for standing by me through the ideas I abandoned or struggled with. You've taught me to believe in myself and to turn my dreams into reality.

To my grandmother Hazel, your gentle spirit has helped shape me into the woman I am today. The moments we've shared echo loudly in my heart. Thank you for always reminding me of my softness & strength.

To my brother Corey, your unwavering support has been a constant in my life. Through every twist and turn, you've reassured me, pushed me and challenged me when I needed it most. Those tough conversations, though not always easy, have been invaluable. Through it all, you've become one of my best friends.

To the man that gives me constant laughter and motivation, Tariq! From the moment we met, you believed in me. This cookbook may be a few years late, but we both know it was worth the wait. As we always say: Do it right, or don't do it at all! Thank you for rolling up your sleeves and working with me in kitchens from state to state. Thank you for being with me every step of the way. My right hand, my go to!

The usual suspects, MY VILLAGE, Nneka, Jenny, Louise, Johnny, Noelle, Olivier, Erin & Tisha. Thank you for the late night chats filled with laughs and ugly cries, I would not stand as strong as I do without your love and kindness. I appreciate your support and I'm extremely grateful to call you friends, more so, my family.

Special thanks to my incredible long-standing clients: Don, Kristen, Susan, Odell & Heather, thank you for welcoming me into your homes, for believing in me, and for trusting in my abilities. Your support means more to me than words can express.

Last but not least, my followers and supporters. Thank you for the warm words, funny comments and always asking for more. Thank you for coming along for the ride.

Love Always, in **ALL WAYS**,

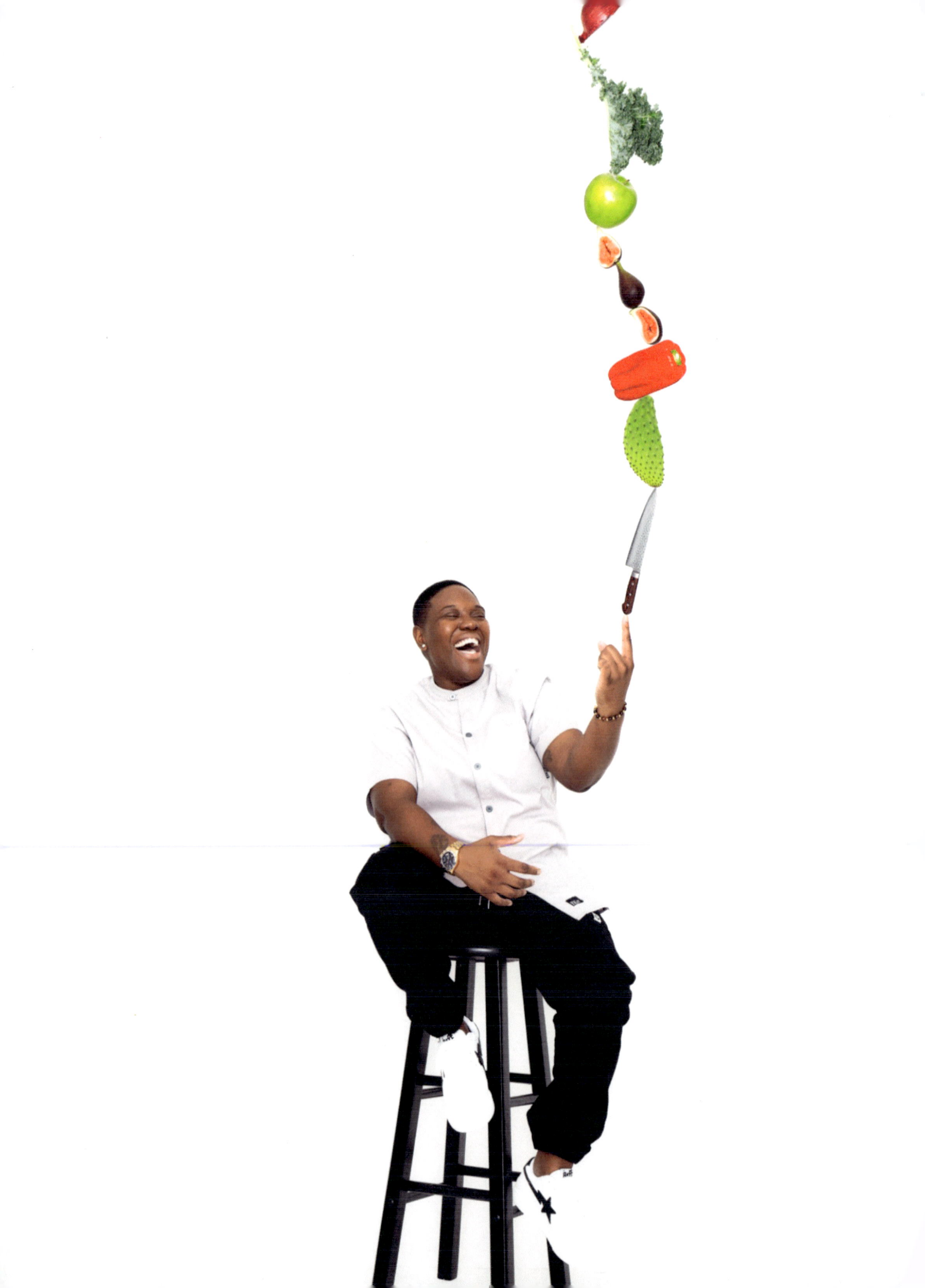

## INDEX

**Beef**
Beef & Broccoli w/ Brown Rice, 117
Dirty Cauliflower Rice, 75
Rib Eye W/ Chimichurri Sauce, 121
The Brooklyn Burger, 55

**Chicken**
Curry Chicken, 127
Infamous Fried Chicken Sando, 56
Roasted Chicken Thighs W/ Tomato Sauce, 119

**Cocktails**
Basil Old Fashioned, 127
East Hampton Paloma, 123
Sorrel Margarita, 125
The Doctors Orders, 121

**Dog Food**
Bleu's Favorite Meal, 130
Peanut Buddy Oat Bites, 138
Quinoa Blueberry Cookies, 134
Sweet Potato Cookies, 136
The Breath Mint, 132

**Fish**
Avocado Toast W/ Smoked Salmon & Ricotta, 21
Branzino W/ Napa Cabbage & Watercress Salad, 115
Chipotle Tunacado, 43
Pan seared Red Snapper, 107
Shakshuka W/ Fried Fish, 33
Swordfish Tacos, 62

**Libations**
The Doctor's orders, 155
The East Hampton Paloma, 157
Tamarind Elderflower Margarita, 159
Sorrel Margarita, 161
Basil Old fashioned, 163

**Bleu Approved Eats**
Bleu's Dinner, 167
The Breath Mint, 169
Quinoa Blueberry Cookies, 171
Sweet Potato Cracker, 173
Peanut Buddy Oat bites, 175

**Grilled Cheese**
The 3am Grilled Cheese, 37

**Lamb**
Braised Lamb Shank W/ Mashed Potato, 125
Grilled Lamb w/ pear & shallot gastrique, 105

**Pasta**
Red Pepper Pasta, 109
Arugula Pesto Pasta, 111
Shrimp Fra Diavolo, 113

**Plantain**
Fried Plantain W/ Rum Butter Glaze, 45
Jerk Mushroom & Sweet Plantain Empanadas, 59

**Pork**
Bacon Egg N Cheese, 17
Quiche Loraine, 23
Henrietta's Ribs, 47
Saturday Morning Kissed Pork Belly, 51

**Salads**
Couscous Salad, 69
Cucumber Nosh, 65
Farro Summer Salad, 71
Spiced Caesar Salad, 67

**Shellfish**
Harissa Curry Ginger Mussels, 123
Salt & Pepper Shrimp, 41
Shrimp Burger, 53

**Soups**
Shrimp Bisque, 81
Curry Lentil Soup, 79
Fortified Fish Sauce w/ Ramen, 83

**Vegan Friendly**
Sweet Potato quinoa tacos, 60
Sneaky Apple pie
Cucumber nosh, 65
Couscous salad, 69
Farro summer salad, 71
Crispy Honey Brussel sprouts, 73
Mushroom fried rice, 77
Curry lentil soup, 79
Arugula pesto pasta, 111
Spiced pineapple mango sorbet, 135
The Doctor's orders, 155
The East Hampton Paloma, 157
Tamarind Elderflower margarita, 159
Basil Old Fashioned, 163
Sorrel margarita, 161

**Sweets**
Bread Pudding W/ Chantilly Cream, 149
Buttermilk Tart, 137
Cam's Banana Bread, 141
Cinnamon Rolls, 19
Dulce De leche beignets, 133
Kissed by Coco, 151
Colleen's Pound Cake, 131
Red Velvet Cake, 139
Sea Salt Chocolate Chip Cookies, 145
Shortbread cookie trifle, 143
Sneaky Apple Pie, 27
Spiced Pineapple Mango Sorbet, 135
The Cookie House Blondies, 147
The Dutch Baby, 29

**Tomato**
Candied Tomato Bruschetta W/ Brown Butter Ricotta, 39

**Vegetables**
Crispy Honey Balsamic Glazed Garlic Brussel Sprouts, 73
Mushroom Fried Rice, 77
Roasted Sweet Potato & Quinoa Tacos, 60
Spanakopita Pie, 49
Sweet Potato Oatmeal Pancakes, 25
The Unforgettable Potato, 35


**ISBN 979-8-218-62705-8**

**Library of Congress Catalog-in-publication Data has been applied for.**
**Cooking / Entertaining**
**Cooking Courses & Dishes / Appetizers**
**Cooking Methods / General**

**Photograph copyright 2025 by Renee Blackman**
**Copyright 2025 Renee Blackman**

To my fellow chefs and cooks, remember the six P's. Proper preparation prevents a piss poor performance.

Made in the USA
Columbia, SC
26 June 2025